# Basic Composition for ESL

## An Expository Workbook

THIRD EDITION

Jann Huizenga

Courtenay Meade Snellings

Gladys Berro Francis

**Scott, Foresman/Little, Brown**
Glenview, Illinois
London, England

*Art by Kim Crowley*

**Library of Congress Cataloging-in-Publication Data**

Huizenga, Jann.
   Basic composition for ESL : an expository workbook / Jann Huizenga, Courtenay Meade Snellings, Gladys Berro Francis. — 3rd ed.
      p.    cm.
   ISBN   0-673-38860-3
   1. English language—Rhetoric—Problems, exercises, etc. 2. English language—Textbooks for foreign speakers. I. Meade-Snellings, Courtenay. II. Francis, Gladys Berro. III. Title.
PE1413.H85   1990
808'.042—dc20

90-33085
CIP

1  2  3  4  5  6  RRW  95  94  93  92  91  90

# Contents

# *Preface*

This writing workbook has been designed for university-bound students or professionals who are studying English as a second language at the advanced-beginning or intermediate level (approximate TOEFL range 320–420). It is flexible enough, however, to be used by any others wanting to improve their basic writing skills. Specifically, the text is intended to be used after students have gained rudimentary competence in writing at the sentence level. It provides material for about sixty class hours of instruction, or a twelve-week writing course.

*Basic Composition for ESL* is rooted in the belief that basic organizational skills and modes of communication *can* and *should* be taught at a very early stage in the nonnative student's writing career; it need not be postponed, as it traditionally has been, until students have a firm grasp of grammar at the sentence level. Students who concentrate from the outset on the grammatical aspects of writing, ignoring writing as organized communication, must often break bad habits in advanced writing courses. Therefore, this text undertakes to develop an *early* approach to writing as coherent, meaningful communication, even though this communication is as yet grammatically simple. Straightforward, step-by-step explanations and exercises guide the student. Six practical and academic writing purposes are covered in six units: *Giving Instructions, Telling What Happened: Objective Reporting, Analyzing by Cause and Effect, Comparing and Contrasting, Classifying,* and *Describing a Mechanism or a Process.*

It is very important that writing assignments offer control at this level, but at the same time, they must provide creative outlets. *Basic Composition for ESL* offers a balance of control and creativity. This situation of "controlled creativity" is set up in the first two sections of each unit by a short prose piece displaying the rhetorical purpose in question, followed first by exercises on organization and grammar and then by a planning and writing assignment that parallels the sample prose piece and for which students receive visual cues. Both the vocabulary and the organizational principles students need to use are similar to those of the sample prose piece. The structure of the picture cues gives students working guidelines. At the same time, however, because of the visual rather than verbal nature of the cues, students feel responsible for generating the sentences. The pictures leave room for student creativity and invention; within guidelines, students can try new lexical items and grammatical structures and expand on the topic by adding their own details. For more secure students, especially, this option to take risks is important. By the third section of each unit, the control gives way to looser guidance; students are encouraged to experiment with what they have learned by writing on one of four suggested unillustrated topics or developing their own topic.

*Basic Composition for ESL* is structured so that the six writing purposes and the general content of the units gradually increase in complexity. Each unit opens with a brief introduction discussing the writing purpose taught in that unit and pointing out its academic and practical use. There are three sections per unit, and each section contains the following segments: Planning, Writing, Organization, Grammar and Punctuation, Student Plan, and Student Composition.

Each section begins with a sample plan (in the form of an outline, an idea map, a chart, or informal notes) followed by a short prose piece illustrating in clear and simple language the rhetorical purpose in question. The topics are diverse and of potential use and interest to foreign students: "How to Feel Comfortable at an American Dinner Party," "The First Manned Flight to the Moon," "Earthquakes," and so on. The Organization segment requires students to actively work with logical relationships, main idea sentences, transitions, and techniques for paragraph development, all of which are introduced here in a simple and structured manner. The Grammar and Punctuation segment treats grammatical structures and punctuation points as they are relevant to the writing purpose in question. Finally, the Student Plan and Student Composition at the end of each section provide students an opportunity to experiment with and consolidate what they have learned. The progression in each unit is from guided to free. In the first section of each unit, student writing is controlled by picture cues. In the second section, students have a choice of following picture cues or of writing an unguided composition (but one nonetheless similar to the section's sample prose piece). The third section allows students, as mentioned above, to write on one of several unguided topics or to develop their own.

This Third Edition continues the attempt begun in the second to put increased emphasis on the process of writing and on the various strategies writers can use in the process. This new edition introduces students to the prewriting strategies of informal note making, idea mapping, and chart making in addition to more formal outlining and encourages more pair and group brainstorming prior to planning and/or writing. Audience concerns are dealt with in more depth as well; all sample prose pieces have been contextualized and made more realistic by including information on who wrote the piece and for what reason. The Stepping Along activities in each Student Composition section, added in the second edition, guide students in the steps of drafting, peer reading, redrafting, and editing. The steps are adaptable and may, of course, be used, omitted, or changed according to students' needs and instructor's preferences. Where students are working on an initial draft, their attention has been drawn primarily to clarity of content and organization. Students should get down the substance of what they want to say before worrying about polishing it. Thus, specific editing activities are left for last and up to the discretion of individual instructors; but for easy reference, a chart of correction symbols that may be used to help students edit their work is included on pages 249–250.

*Basic Composition for ESL* has several other important features. The numerous illustrations throughout enliven the text and can be used effectively to elicit oral production in a preoutlining and/or writing phase. A glossary at the end of the book provides simple definitions and examples of terms used within the text. Finally, the accompanying *Instructor's Manual*—which can be ordered with the student book from Scott, Foresman and Company—provides an answer key for the instructor's convenience, detailed comments on general and specific ways to use the text, discussion of problems that may arise, and suggestions for the correction of student compositions.

We appreciate the helpful input of our colleagues and students over the past few years. We are grateful to reviewers Jane Curtis of Roosevelt University and Dolores Mirabella of South Seattle Community College for their many suggestions.

We thank our editors Roseanne Mendoza, Elaine Goldberg, and Diane Beausoleil for their careful attention to this manuscript. Artist Kim Crowley deserves special thanks for his fine illustrations.

Finally, gratitude is due to our families, whose patience and support are deeply appreciated. We particularly thank our husbands, Kim, Bill, and Vic, for sharing their general and technical knowledge with us.

# Introduction

The aim of this book is to teach you some basic points about writing. Knowing how to express ideas in writing in an organized way is important for everybody, but it is especially important for you as a student or professional. By the time you finish this book, you will have mastered the basic steps of the writing process and will be able to write compositions for six practical and academic purposes.

## What is a composition?

A composition is a piece of writing about one central topic. It may consist of one or more paragraphs. If the central topic is broad and needs to be divided into several subtopics, each of these subtopics should be developed in at least one paragraph. For instance, if you want to discuss types of food, you may want to break your central topic down into four subtopics: meat, dairy products, fruits and vegetables, and grains. You might use, then, a separate paragraph for each subtopic. A composition of more than one paragraph usually has an introduction and a conclusion that are separate paragraphs.

## What is a paragraph?

A **paragraph** is a group of related sentences that communicates one central idea. A paragraph may be short or long according to the simplicity or complexity of the subject.

## What does a paragraph look like?

The first line of a paragraph is indented in most kinds of writing. This means that you must leave an empty space to show the beginning of the paragraph. A composition that has one paragraph will have only one indentation. A composition that has two paragraphs will have two indentations, and so on. Make sure that you capitalize the first word in each sentence and end each sentence with a period (.), question mark (?), or exclamation point (!). If your paragraph is a composition, put your title at the top of the page.

Put the title on the top line. →

Indent your paragraph. →

Capitalize the first word in each sentence. →

End each sentence with a period. →

Write *on* the lines. ↕

*Why Accidents Occur*

*Automobile accidents occur for a variety of reasons. First, poor weather conditions are often responsible. When the roads are snowy, icy, or wet, it is more difficult to control a car. Accidents can also happen when certain parts of the automobile malfunction. Faulty brakes and defective tires, for example, have been blamed for many mishaps. But the most common cause of accidents is driver error. A careless, sleepy, or drunk driver is not fully alert and runs a high risk of having an accident.*

## How does a paragraph begin?

A paragraph usually begins with a general statement. We call this general statement the main idea sentence, though it is sometimes called a topic sentence. The main idea sentence tells the reader what the paragraph is about and limits the kind of information that should be included in the paragraph. The main idea sentence is usually the first sentence of the paragraph, but experienced writers sometimes place it in the middle or at the end of the paragraph.

## How does a paragraph progress?

The main idea sentence is followed by **major points.** The major points are the sentences that explain the main idea sentence. They give more information about it. Below, the major points of the paragraph are in italics. They are expanded with additional details.

Automobile accidents occur for a variety of reasons. *First, poor weather conditions are often responsible.* When the roads are snowy, icy, or wet, it is more difficult to control a car. *Accidents can also happen when certain parts of the automobile malfunction.* Faulty brakes and defective tires, for example, have been blamed for many mishaps. *But the most common cause of accidents is driver error.* A careless, sleepy, or drunk driver is not fully alert and runs a high risk of having an accident.

## What holds a paragraph together?

Ideas in a paragraph are often connected with **transitions.** Transitions show the relationship between these ideas. Transitions include words and phrases such as *first, finally, in addition, for example,* and *in contrast.* Without transitions, your paragraph will not read smoothly. You will learn to use different kinds of transitions for different purposes. Transitions are also used to connect paragraphs.

# Unit 1
# *Giving Instructions*

In this unit, you will practice writing clear instructions. When you give instructions, you explain how to do something. You are giving instructions when you tell someone how to cook a chicken, how to get downtown, or how to change a tire. In academic and professional situations, it is often necessary to explain clearly in writing how to do something. You might need to explain, for example, how to conduct a chemical experiment, how to diagnose a certain illness, or how to program a new computer. There are several important points to remember when you write instructions.

1. *Use chronological order.* First and most important, when you tell someone how to do something, remember to write the steps for the process in exact order, just as you do them. If you are explaining how to cook a chicken, for example, you need to tell how to clean it before you tell how to season it.

2. *Keep your audience in mind.* You must decide before you begin to write whom the instructions will be for. A city resident and a tourist will not need the same directions for going downtown.

3. *Be clear.* Explain your instructions clearly. Keep your sentences short. If they are confusing, your reader may not be able to follow your directions correctly.

4. *Be thorough.* Explain each step carefully—not only *what* to do but *how* to do it. For example, when explaining how to change a tire, don't just tell your reader to raise the car. Instead, explain exactly how high to raise it and what tool to use.

5. *Be exact.* Make sure your facts and details are precise. If you are giving directions, say, "Go twelve blocks" instead of "Go about half a mile."

6. *Stick to the point.* Be sure all the information you include is related to your main purpose. When telling how to change a tire, don't discuss where to buy cheap tires or how long new ones should last. Such details may interest the reader, but they won't help in changing the tire.

7. *Be complete.* Be very careful not to leave out any steps. Remember, you know how to do what you are explaining, but your reader might not.

# 1
## *How to Feel Comfortable at an American Dinner Party*

## PLANNING

A student from Brazil wants to give some advice in a foreign-student newsletter about behavior at dinner parties in the U.S. Before writing, she made this *outline* of her ideas.

1. Buy a small gift.
2. Be on time!
3. Compliment your host.
4. Don't stay too long!
5. Say thank you.

It is often useful to plan before you begin to write. Planning will help you organize your thoughts. One type of plan is an **outline** like this one. When you write an outline, you make a list of your **major points.** If you are going to give instructions, your major points will be listed in **chronological order**—you will tell what should be done first, second, third, and so on.

## WRITING

This is the student's final **draft.** How is it different from the outline? *Circle the words or phrases that show chronological order.*

> ## How to Feel Comfortable at an American Dinner Party
>
> Feeling comfortable at an American dinner party is not difficult if you follow these instructions. First, you should buy a small gift such as flowers, candy, or wine for your host or hostess. Second, arrive on time. If the dinner engagement is for 7:00, don't arrive after 7:15 without calling. Next, during dinner, be sure to compliment your host or hostess on the meal. After you finish eating, you should not stay more than a few hours. Finally, thank your host or hostess for the dinner when you leave.

## ORGANIZATION

### Main Idea Sentences

The main idea, or main point, of a composition is contained in the main idea sentence. This sentence tells the reader what you are writing about in general. You should write your main idea sentence at the beginning of your composition. (When you become a more experienced writer, you may learn other techniques.) Your explanation and specific examples will follow. *Underline the main idea sentence in the composition above.*

A main idea sentence for a composition that gives instructions tells (1) what the instructions will cover, (2) that the necessary steps for this process will follow, and (3) (optional) why the reader might be interested in reading further.

#### <u>EXAMPLES</u>

Note how the following examples show the above points.

*If you want to get a driver's license, follow these steps.*

*The city library has a good collection of books, and you can get a library card in twenty-four hours by following these directions.*

## Exercise 1A

Circle the best main idea sentence for each of the following paragraphs.

1.     **a.** Deciding what kind of phone you want is not difficult.

       (**b.**) In order to get a phone, follow these directions.

       **c.** If you want to get a phone for the first time, you need to pay a small deposit.

First, you should call the telephone company. Give the company representative your name and address. Next, explain what kind of service and what kind of phone you want. Send a deposit if you have never had a phone before. Someone at the phone company will then arrange a convenient time to have the phone installed.

2.     **a.** You need a frying pan and a spatula to make a cheese omelet.

       **b.** I often make cheese omelets in the following way because they are good.

       (**c.**) A cheese omelet is delicious for breakfast, lunch, or dinner, and you will have no trouble making one if you follow these steps.

First, crack two eggs into a bowl. Add two tablespoons of milk or water and a little salt and pepper. Beat the mixture well with a fork. Then you should melt a tablespoon of butter in a small frying pan and pour the egg mixture into the pan. Cook on medium-high heat for five minutes. When the omelet becomes firm on the bottom, lay thin slices of cheese on it. Cook it a minute longer. Then fold it in half with a spatula. Finally, carefully remove the omelet from the pan and serve it.

3.     **a.** If you want to send a package from the U.S., you must go to the post office.

       (**b.**) Sending a package from the U.S. is not difficult if you follow these simple instructions.

       **c.** If you want a package to arrive at its destination fast, send it first class.

First, wrap your package well. Print the receiver's address in the middle of the package and your address in the upper-left-hand corner. Then go to the post office. Go up to one of the windows, and give your package to the clerk. You should tell the clerk whether you want it to go first, third, or fourth class (second class is used only for newspapers and periodicals) and if you want to insure it. Finally, pay your money.

## Transitions Showing Chronological Order

When you write, you want your reader to follow you easily as you move from one part of your composition to another. We often use transitions to help the reader see the relationship between the parts. When giving instructions, you will want to use transitions that show the *time* relationship between the steps. These transitions include the following:

First, . . . (Second, Third, and so on)

Next, . . .

Then . . .

Finally/Lastly, . . .

Commas are usually used after all the above transitions except *Then*. Use these words carefully. Too many transitions might make your composition monotonous. *Did you find the transitions in the composition on page 3?*

### Exercise 1B

Below are main idea sentences followed by four sentences. Place the sentences in proper chronological order by numbering them. Then rewrite all sentences in paragraph form, choosing words from the group of transitions. Don't use more than three transitions.

1.    If you need to take a taxi in New York City, follow these steps.

    _3_   Tell the driver where you want to go.

    _1_   Step into the street and flag one down.

    _4_   Pay and tip the driver upon arrival.

    _2_   Get in the back seat.

*If you need to take a taxi in New York City, follow these steps. Step into the street and flag one down. Ge in the back seat. Thell the driver where you want to go. Pay and tip the driver upon arrival*

2.    Traveler's checks are a safe way to carry money when traveling, and you can purchase them in the following manner.

    _2_   Ask a teller to give you the desired amount of checks.

    _4_   Sign your name once in the appropriate spot on each check before you leave the bank.

    _1_   Go to your local bank.

    _3_   Pay your money plus a small service charge.

# GRAMMAR AND PUNCTUATION

## The Imperative

The imperative form of the verb is used to give instructions, to make requests, and to give orders. You will use this form frequently when you write instructions. The imperative consists of the base form of the verb without a subject pronoun. To make the imperative negative, put *do not* or *don't* before the verb.

### EXAMPLES

Finally, *thank* your host or hostess for the dinner.
*Be* sure to compliment your host or hostess on the meal.

*Don't arrive* after 7:15 without telephoning.
After you finish eating, *do not stay* more than a few hours.

*Note:*   Many of the sentences in the outline of Composition 1 are imperative.

## Exercise 1C

Using the following pictures, imagine you are telling a fifteen-year-old how to take a plane for the first time. Use the imperative form.

Helpful vocabulary:

check luggage (equipaje)

board a plane

flight attendant

1. Find the ticket counter.

3. Go to the Gate and wait

2. Check up your luggage

4.

### Exercise 1D

Imagine you are telling your friend what *not* to do. Use the following pictures to write negative commands.

1. *Please don't smoke.*

2. Please, don't enter

3. Please don't take pictures

4. Please don't sit

*Should*

You just learned how to give your reader instructions using the imperative form. You can also use *should* or *should not (shouldn't)* for this purpose. *Should* is followed by the base form of a verb.

### EXAMPLES

*You should buy* a small gift for your host or hostess.

After you finish eating, *you should not stay* more than a few hours.

### Exercise 1E

I have several problems. Tell me what I should or shouldn't do in the following situations.

1.    I have a bad toothache.

*You should see a dentist right away.*
*You shouldn't eat so much candy!*

2.    I'm gaining too much weight.

You should go on a diet.
You should not eat a lot of sweets.

3.    I want to learn Spanish as quickly as possible.

You should take Espanish class.
You shouldn't speak English.

4.    I'm living far from my family and friends, and I'm very homesick.

You should move close to your family
You shouldn't stay home by yourself

5.    I'm having a hard time making new friends in this city.

You should be friendly
You shouldn't be nasty / rude

## Using *Before*, *After*, and *When* to Show Order

When we give instructions, we often use dependent clauses beginning with *before*, *after*, or *when* to show the sequence of steps. A **clause** is a group of words that contains a subject and a verb. There are two kinds of clauses: main clauses and dependent clauses. A **main** clause can be a separate sentence. A **dependent** clause, however, depends on a main clause for its complete meaning and cannot be a sentence by itself. Each of the following sentences contains a main clause and a dependent clause. *Underline the dependent clause in each.*

Thank your host or hostess for the dinner when you leave.

After you finish eating, do not stay more than a few hours.

Make an appointment before you go to the office.

### EXAMPLES

The following examples show you how *before* and *after* are used to combine two imperative clauses. Notice that the subject *(you)* appears in the dependent clause. If the dependent clause comes first, it is separated from the main clause by a comma.

1. Add the rest of the ingredients.
2. Beat the mixture.

> *After* you add the rest of the ingredients, beat the mixture.
> Beat the mixture *after* you add the rest of the ingredients.

> *Before* you beat the mixture, add the rest of the ingredients.
> Add the rest of the ingredients *before* you beat the mixture.

*When* indicates that two steps occur at the same time.

> *When* you leave, thank your host or hostess.
> Thank your host or hostess *when* you leave.

### Exercise 1F

Punctuate the following sentences where necessary.

1.    After you check your luggage, go directly to the gate.

2.    Before the taxi comes, make sure you have enough money.

3.    Get off the bus, after it has come to a complete stop.

4.    When you reach your destination, pay and tip the taxi driver.

5.    Buy your ticket before you board the plane.

6.    Before the plane takes off, fasten your seat belt.

### Exercise 1G

Now combine the sentences with the words in parentheses. Write each sentence two ways.

1.    Put your books away.
      Begin your test.    (*before*)

*Before you begin your test, put your books away.*
*Put your books away before you begin your test.*

2.    Buy your movie ticket.
      Find a seat.    (*after*)

After you buy your movie ticket, find a seat
Find a seat, after you buy your movie ticket

3.    Arrive at the exam.
      Remain silent.    (*when*)
      silencioso

When you arrive at the exam, Remain silent
Remain silent, when you arrive at the exam.

4.    Do stretching exercises.
      Begin to jog.    (*before*)

Before you begin to job, do stretching exercises.
Do stretching exercises before you begin to jog.

5.    Pick up the telephone receiver.
      Drop twenty-five cents in the coin slot.    (*after*)

Pick up the telephone receiver after Drop twenty-
five cents in the coin slot.

## Punctuation with Items in a Series

Commas are used to separate items in a series. These items may be words, phrases, or clauses. Do not use a comma if only two items are mentioned.

#### EXAMPLES

Buy a small gift such as flowers, candy, or wine.

Baseball, football, tennis, and golf are popular sports in the U.S.

She thanked the host and hostess. (no comma needed)

## Exercise 1H

Punctuate these sentences correctly. Note that some sentences do not need additional punctuation.

1. You will need matches, newspapers, twigs, and logs to make a good fire.

2. He bought milk and bread.

3. They will take a vacation in June, July or August.

4. Mandarin, English, Russian Spanish, and Hindi all have over 200 million speakers.

5. The three most popular natural sites in the U.S. are the Grand Canyon, Yellowstone, National Park, and Niagara Falls.

6. Bring a pen or a sharp pencil to the test.

7. Eggs, celery, onions, and mayonnaise are the ingredients you will need to make a good egg salad.

8. The hikers took canned food a small tent and sleeping bags on their hike.

9. She hopes to visit the Middle East, South America, or Australia next year.

# Student Plan 1
## How to Make a Good Impression at a Job Interview

Imagine that a friend is job hunting. You want to give this friend advice on how to make a good impression at a job interview. The following pictures give you some ideas about how to make a favorable impression.

    With a partner or a small group, discuss the ideas in the pictures. Add more ideas if you can. Then together or individually, write an outline of your ideas. Use the imperative or *should* in your sentences.

**Helpful vocabulary:**

| | |
|---|---|
| library | be polite/be courteous |
| learn about/investigate | answer in detail |
| wear | show interest in |
| interviewer | |

*Main idea sentence** <u>To Make a good Impression at a Job</u>
<u>Interview is easy if you follow this steps.</u>

_____

_____

*You may want to write your main idea sentence after you finish the plan.

you should read the history of the block Company

you should wear a formal dress

Be polite with the interviewer.

Answer in detail every question

Show interest in the job.

Say thank you

# Student Composition 1
## How to Make a Good Impression at a Job Interview

### Stepping Along

**Step 1:**  Use your main idea sentence and your outline to help you write a one-paragraph composition. Use appropriate transitions. Look at Composition 1 on page 3 or the exercises if you need extra help.

**Step 2:**  Exchange paragraphs with a partner. As you read your partner's composition, think about these questions.

- Is everything in your partner's instructions clear to you?

- Did your partner indent the paragraph?

- Does your partner use good transitions with correct punctuation?

- Can you give your partner any suggestions for improvement?

**Step 3:**  Talk with your partner about your paragraphs. Try to agree on improvements that you can make.

**Step 4:**  Rewrite your composition, making any changes you feel are necessary.

**Further steps:**   As directed by your instructor.

# 2
# *How to Use a Copying Machine*

## PLANNING

A student is going to explain in writing how to use a copying machine. First, she thinks about the steps in the process. *Use the pictures and complete her notes.* (Work in pairs or small groups).

| | |
|---|---|
| | 1. Get your money ready. |
| | 2. Turn on the machine. |
| | 3. Set the page-length control. |
| | 4. Set the light/dark control. |
| | 5. Lift the cover. |
| | 6. Place your original on the glass. |
| | 7. Put your money in the coin slot. |
| | 8. Push the start-print |
| | 9. Put it off |
| | 10. remove your book or paper |

## WRITING

Here is her final draft. How is it different from her outline? *Circle the words that she uses to connect the steps.* Is a transition used at the beginning of each sentence? Why not?

### How to Use a Copying Machine

Most copying machines work in a similar way, and they are easy to use if you do the following things. First, you should find out the cost of each copy and get your money ready. Then turn on the machine. Set the page-length control and the light/dark control. Next, lift the cover and place your book or paper facedown on the glass. Put your money in the coin slot. Then press the "start print" button. After your copy comes out in the copy tray, turn off the machine. Finally, don't forget to lift the cover and remove your book or paper.

# ORGANIZATION

### Irrelevant Sentences

A main idea sentence is a general statement that immediately tells the reader the topic, or subject, of the composition. All other sentences in the composition should support or directly relate to the main idea sentence. A sentence is **irrelevant** if it does not directly relate to the main idea sentence. Below is a paragraph containing an irrelevant sentence. It has been crossed out.

#### EXAMPLE

Fresh orange juice tastes better than frozen orange juice, and it can be made in the following way. First, buy some very fresh oranges. ~~Oranges are grown in areas with warm climates.~~ Next, cut the oranges in half. Squeeze the halves in a juicer until all the juice is out. Then throw away the seeds and the pulp. Finally, add a little sugar if you wish, and drink.

### Exercise 2A

In each of the following short compositions, one sentence does not relate to the main idea sentence. Find this irrelevant sentence and cross it out.

1.     Following these simple rules may help you find an apartment in a new city. First, if you have friends in the area, ask them if they know of any vacant apartments. If you don't know anyone in the area, look in the classified ads in the newspaper under Apartments for Rent. You can also find job announcements and cars for sale in the classified ads. Then make phone calls to the apartments that look good to you. If you have no success, look in the phone book under Real Estate. Call as many real estate offices as you can, and ask if they have any apartments available. Finally, after you get a list of rentals from these offices, go to see the apartments and choose the one you like.

2.     You can treat first- and second-degree burns yourself by following these simple instructions: First, immerse the burn in cold water until the pain subsides. Next, dry the burn gently with a sterile gauze pad or a clean cloth. Do not put any pressure on it. When the burn is completely dry, cover it loosely with a dry bandage. Then, if an arm or a leg is burned, raise it higher than the heart. Finally, call a doctor if necessary. Remember that burns often result from carelessness.

3.     Cooking hamburgers outdoors is not difficult if you follow these directions. First, put charcoal on an outdoor grill. Wet the charcoal thoroughly with lighter fluid. Next, light a match and ignite the coals. After starting the fire, wait about thirty minutes until the coals begin to turn gray. Then put the raw hamburger patties on the grill. Sprinkle them with salt and pepper. You should also sprinkle steak, chicken, and pork chops with salt and pepper when you grill them. Turn the hamburgers over after about ten minutes. Cook them for another ten minutes and eat immediately.

## GRAMMAR AND PUNCTUATION

### Using *And* to Join Two Sentences

Two independent clauses that are related may be joined with *and*. A comma comes before *and* unless the clauses are very short.

#### EXAMPLE

Most copying machines work in a similar way, *and* they are easy to use if you do the following things.

### Exercise 2B

Join the sentences using *and*. Punctuate correctly.

1.  First put the charcoal on the grill. Then wet it with lighter fluid.

    *First, put the charcoal on the grill, and then wet it with lighter fluid.*

2.  Go to your local bank. Ask a teller to give you the desired amount of checks.

    Go to your local bank, and Ask a teller to give you the desired amount of checks.

3.  Tacos can be made inexpensively. They can also be prepared easily.

    Tacos can be made inexpensively and they can also be prepared easily.

4.  Place the paper facedown on the glass. Put your money in the coin slot.

    Place the paper facedown on the glass and put your money in the coin slot.

5.  Cut fresh oranges in half. Squeeze them in a juicer until all the juice is out.

    Cut fresh oranges in half and squeeze them in juicer until all the juice is out.

Exercise 2C    Review of *Before* and *After*

Combine the following sentences two ways using the word in parentheses. Omit *then* when you rewrite the sentences.

1.     Set the page-length control. Then set the light/dark control.     *(after)*

> *After you set the page-length control, set the light/dark control.*
>
> *Set the light/dark control after you set the page-length control.*

2.     Turn on the machine. Then set the page-length control.     *(before)*

3.     Place the book or paper facedown on the glass. Then put your money in the coin slot.     *(after)*

4.     Lift the cover. Then remove your book or paper.     *(before)*

5.     Set the light/dark control. Then lift the cover.     *(after)*

# Student Plan 2
## How to Use a Machine

A. Make an outline to write about any machine that you are familiar with.

OR

B. Imagine that someone you know has left home to go to college and must use a Laundromat for the first time.

   With a partner or a small group, discuss the pictures. Can you add suggestions of your own? Use these pictures and your own ideas to write an outline for a set of instructions on how to use a commercial washing machine. Use the imperative or *should* in your sentences.

### Helpful vocabulary:

| | |
|---|---|
| load | water-temperature control |
| lid | fabric-selection control |
| measure | laundry |
| pour into/add | |

*Main idea sentence\** _____

_____

_____

*You may want to write your main idea sentence after you finish the plan.

# Student Composition 2
## How to Use a Machine

### Stepping Along

**Step 1:** Use your main idea sentence and your outline to help you write a one-paragraph composition. Use *before* and *after*, once each, as well as other appropriate transitions. Look at the composition on page 17 or the exercises if you need help.

**Step 2:** Exchange compositions with a partner. As you read your partner's composition, think about these questions.

- Suppose that you had never used this machine. Would you be able to operate one with your partner's instructions?

- Has your partner omitted any steps?

- Are all the instructions clear?

- Are transitions used correctly?

- Can you give your partner suggestions for improvement?

**Step 3:** Talk with your partner about your paragraphs. Try to agree on improvements that you can make.

**Step 4:** Rewrite your composition, making any changes you feel are necessary.

**Further steps:** As directed by your instructor.

# *3*

# *How to Get to Arlington National Cemetery from the White House*

## PLANNING

Hirofumi Ano lives in Washington, D.C. He is helping to plan a class trip to the White House and Arlington National Cemetery. He wants to write directions for his classmates who are driving from the White House to the cemetery. Before writing, he looks at a map and thinks of the steps. He didn't finish his outline. *Can you complete it looking at the map?* Work with a partner if you wish.

1. Find The Zero Milestone (on the Ellipse Road).
2. Drive halfway around The Ellipse.
3. Turn left on The access road to Constitution Ave.
4. Go right on Constitution.
5. Drive *west* to 23rd St.
6. Turn left.
7. Enter The traffic circle (around Lincoln Memorial).

## WRITING

These are Hirofumi's directions in paragraph form. How is the paragraph different from his outline? *Circle the transitions he uses.*

You can get from the White House to Arlington National Cemetery in eight to ten minutes if you follow these directions. First, you should find the Zero Milestone on The Ellipse road south of the White House. After that, drive halfway around The Ellipse, and turn left on the short access road to Constitution Avenue. You will see the Washington Monument in front of you. Then go right at Constitution Avenue. Drive west along Constitution to 23rd Street. Turn left and continue along 23rd Street until you enter the traffic circle around the Lincoln Memorial. Take the exit ramp to Arlington Memorial Bridge over the Potomac River. At the end of the bridge, there is another traffic circle. Continue halfway around the circle, and take the exit road to Arlington National Cemetery. It will be a half mile down this road.

# ORGANIZATION

## Transitions Showing Chronological Order

The transition *after that* (found in Composition 3) is used in the same way as *next* and *then*—to show that one event follows another. None of these words is used to connect two sentences.

Check your luggage. $\begin{cases} \textit{After that,} \\ \textit{Next,} \\ \textit{Then} \end{cases}$ go to the gate.

*After* and *before*, however, are used to connect two sentences.

> *After* you check your luggage, go to the gate.
> *Before* you go to the gate, check your luggage.

### Exercise 3A

Using the word or words in parentheses, rewrite the following sentences to show clearly the time relationship between them.

1.  **a.** Go over the bridge.

    **b.** Bear right onto Green Street.      (*after that*)

    _____

    _____

2.  **a.** Turn left onto Green Street.

    **b.** Drive a half block to Garden Vista Apartments.      (*after*)

    _____

    _____

3.  **a.** Drive halfway around the traffic circle.

    **b.** Go right at Virginia Avenue.      (*then*)

    _____

    _____

4.  **a.** Turn right onto Park Street.

    **b.** Drive a half mile to King's Highway.      (*next*)

    _____

    _____

5.  **a.** Go over the bridge.

    **b.** Start looking for the exit ramp to Arlington National Cemetery.      (*before*)

    _____

    _____

Exercise 3B   Main Idea Sentences

Write main idea sentences for the paragraphs below.

1. _It is not difficut to make fire if you follow this instructions._ _(in a fire place.)_

   _If you want to make a fire in your fireplace follow these four steps._

First, put crumpled _(arrugadas)_ pieces of newspaper in the fireplace. Lay twigs or small pieces of wood on top of the newspaper. Then put two or three logs on top. Finally, light the newspaper with a match, and you will soon have a beautiful fire. — _Topic = fire — How to make fire._

2. _Cleannig windows is easy if you follow this steps._

   _____

   _____

First, find a bucket or a large bowl and a sponge. Fill the bucket with water, and add about a cup of ammonia. Then wet the sponge and wipe the window clean. Finally, dry it well with a paper towel. Your window will shine.

3. _____

   _____

   _____

   _____

First, take the cap off the gas tank. Then turn the lever on the gas pump to ON. Put the nozzle in the tank. When you have the amount of gas you want, return the nozzle to the pump. Turn the lever to OFF before paying the attendant.

# GRAMMAR AND PUNCTUATION

## Showing Directions with *Go*, *Drive*, and *Walk*

There are many prepositions and adverbs that can follow the verbs *go*, *drive*, and *walk*. Some of them are explained by the following diagrams.

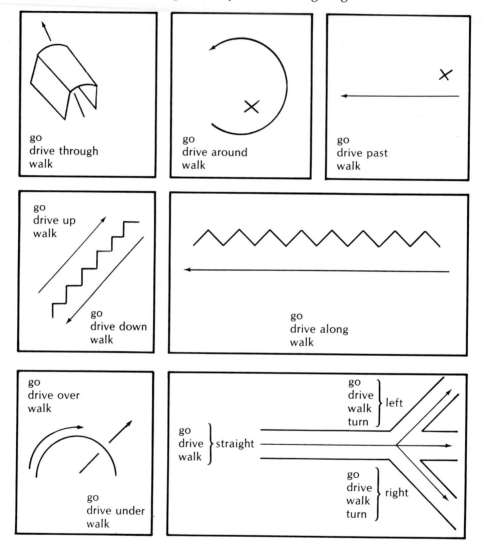

## Exercise 3C

Tell your friend how to find the admissions office in this imaginary campus. Write an imperative sentence with *go* for each arrow. Put your instructions in chronological order.

1. *Go through the main entrance.*

2.

3.

4.

5.

6.

## Exercise 3D   Review of Punctuation

Punctuate the following sentences correctly by adding commas. Some need no punctuation.

1. After you finish the experiment put away the chemicals.

2. New York Los Angeles and Chicago are the three largest cities in the United States.

3. Second lay out all necessary materials.

4. Make reservations before you go to a popular restaurant on a Saturday night.

5. The English words *silk tea catsup* and *tycoon* originally come from Chinese.

6. Be sure to thank your host or hostess when you leave.

7. Next add a cup of buttermilk or sour cream to the mixture.

8. Before you come to the exam get a good night's rest.

9. When the mail arrives open it if you wish.

10. You can buy money orders and traveler's checks at your local bank.

# Student Plan and Composition 3

Develop your own topic, or choose one of the topics below for a final composition that gives instructions.

1. Imagine that a friend is visiting you from out of town and that she has to drive somewhere. Tell her, for example, how to get to a specific theater or to the airport from your home.

2. Imagine that you are having a party and that you invited your classmate. Tell him how to get to your apartment from the university or college.

3. Explain to your teacher how to make a favorite drink or food from your country (Turkish coffee, Chinese chicken, and so on). Your teacher will probably want to try your recipe, so make your instructions very clear! Be very specific about amounts of ingredients and length of cooking time.

4. *MORE CHALLENGING:* Imagine that a friend of yours who knows very little English has just arrived in the United States. Your friend wants to learn English as quickly as possible, but she or he doesn't know where to begin and how to proceed. Tell your friend what you think she or he should do first, second, third, and so on.

## Stepping Along

**Step 1:** After choosing your topic, work in pairs, and take turns giving your instructions to each other orally. Ask questions of each other when something is not clear. Remember that you are helping your partner by asking him or her to be specific.

**Step 2:** On your own, make an outline with a main idea sentence. Be complete, and put your steps in chronological order.

**Step 3:** Exchange outlines with the same partner. Can you follow your partner's instructions? Has your partner omitted any steps? Discuss your outlines together.

**Step 4:** Write your instructions in paragraph form. Use appropriate transitions (*first, next, and so on*) and punctuate correctly.

**Step 5:** Exchange compositions with a new partner. As you read your partner's composition, think about these questions.

- What do you like best about the composition?
- Are all the instructions clear?
- Are transitions used correctly?
- Is the punctuation correct?
- Can you give your partner any suggestions for improvement?

**Step 6:** Talk with your partner about the strong and weak points of your compositions. Try to agree on improvements that you can make.

**Step 7:** Rewrite your composition, making any changes you feel are necessary.

**Further steps:** As directed by your instructor.

# Unit 2
## Telling What Happened: Objective Reporting

In this unit, you will learn how to write an **objective report.** An objective report is an organized presentation of facts. Its purpose is to tell someone about something that happened. There are many different types of reports, and they are used in many different situations. When we read the newspaper, for example, we read reports of accidents, fires, and political events. When the sports newscaster on television tells us what happened in the baseball game between the Philadelphia Phillies and the New York Mets, the newscaster is reporting. When you tell your fellow students what occurred at the foreign-student meeting you attended, you are reporting. You will write good objective reports if you remember the following:

1. *Follow chronological order.* You have already learned to follow chronological order when you give instructions. When you write a report, you should follow this same order; tell what happened first, what happened next, and so on.

2. *Be precise.* Being precise means being *exact.* You should give exact information—exact names, times, and places. For example, when writing a report on a chemical experiment in the laboratory, you should not say, "I filled a test tube half full with water and added a little sugar," but rather, "I filled a test tube half full with water and added three grams of sugar." In a report on the history of Ghana, you should not say, "Ghana became a republic sometime in 1960," but, "Ghana became a republic on July 1, 1960."

3. *Be objective.* Being objective means keeping your opinion out of the report. Because the purpose of a report is to tell what happened, it should not include your own feelings about the events. For example, when writing a report on an accident in a nuclear power plant, you should not say, "This accident proves that all nuclear power plants should be closed." This might be your point of view, but it should not be included in the factual account of the accident.

4. *Be accurate.* Being accurate means that all dates, numbers, names, and other information in the report must be correct. For example, if you are writing a report on the life of John F. Kennedy, but you are not sure of his birth date, you should check your information in a reliable sourcebook.

The ability to write good reports will be useful to you as students and professionals. As a history student, for instance, you might be asked to report on the events surrounding the signing of the United Nations Charter in 1945. As a business executive, you might want to report on what happened during an important company meeting. Or, as an engineer, you might need to write a report telling what occurred during the construction of a hydroelectric power plant. These kinds of reports are more sophisticated than those that you will write in this unit, but the same principles apply.

# 4
## Ice Causes Accident

## PLANNING

A reporter of a small-town newspaper visited the scene of a car accident and took these notes while speaking with the driver and the police.

## WRITING

Her report appeared like this the next day. *Underline the main idea sentence. Circle the words and phrases that show time order.*

### ICE CAUSES ACCIDENT

Yesterday, Mary Chan, town council member, had an accident near the corner of Main and Lincoln. At 10:00 A.M., she was driving down Main Street with a passenger, Jane Fields, in the snow. At Lincoln Avenue, she turned right, and the car skidded on a patch of ice. First, she hit the car of Joseph Schwartz. Then she hit a tree. Moments later, the police arrived. Both Ms. Chan and Ms. Fields reported that they were not injured, but the driver of the other car, Mr. Schwartz, told police that his neck hurt. The police took him to Fairfield General Hospital for examination.

# ORGANIZATION

## Chronological Order

When you are reporting, your information should be arranged in chronological order: you should tell what happened first, what happened next, and so on.

### Exercise 4A

The following sentences tell about a fire, but they are not in chronological order. Number them in the proper order.

_____ **a.** Five fire fighters arrived at the scene at 5:07 A.M.

_____ **b.** They fought the blaze for half an hour.

_____ **c.** Police reported that the fire caused $8,000 worth of damage.

__1__ **d.** The fire at the Cambridge Apartments was first noticed at 5:00 A.M. by Mr. Carl Sims, who called the fire department.

_____ **e.** They then broke the windows and brought their hoses in.

_____ **f.** The fire fighters immediately awakened and evacuated all residents of the apartment building.

## Main Idea Sentences

A main idea sentence for a report should tell the reader (1) *what* particular event is being reported, (2) *who or what* was involved, (3) *where* the event happened, and (4) *when* it happened.

### EXAMPLES

Read the following examples of main idea sentences for reports. Does each sentence contain the necessary information for a good main idea setence?

*Three thousand runners participated in the annual Great Race, which was held in Pittsburgh on June 2.*

*On October 16, 1934, Mao Tse-tung and his Red Army began their Long March near Fukein, China.*

*Carnegie-Mellon University held its homecoming on Saturday, October 13, on the campus.*

*William Lee of 318 Linden Street was seriously injured in an automobile accident on Route 81 early Monday morning.*

### Exercise 4B

Read the following reports. Circle the best main idea sentence for each.

1.  a. Virginia Lipsky won the first prize last Monday.

    b. Seventy cyclists rode through Gateway Park on October 10.

    c. On October 10, seventy cyclists participated in the Schwinn Bicycle Race in Wilton, Oregon.

    At 8:00 A.M., the cyclists began to gather at the starting line in Gateway Park. The race began at 9:00 A.M. The cyclists rode down Ardmore Boulevard through the park and on to Ellisville, which is forty miles (64 kilometers) south of Wilton. At 10:41 A.M., the first cyclist, Virginia Lipsky, crossed the finish line and was awarded the $100 first prize.

2.  a. Last Monday evening, two men robbed the home of Juan Lopez of Kentwood Avenue.

    b. Two men took Juan Lopez's television set.

    c. Last Monday, the police arrived at Juan Lopez's home at 1:20 A.M.

    At 1:00 A.M., Mr. Lopez was sleeping upstairs when he heard noises downstairs. He went downstairs and saw two masked men going out the front door with his television set. He waited until they had left, and then he called the police. They arrived at 1:20 A.M. Mr. Lopez gave them a description of the two men and filled out a crime report. The criminals have not yet been caught.

3.  a. On August 21, 1911, Vincenzo Perruggia stole a painting from the Louvre.

    b. The Mona Lisa, one of the most famous paintings in the world, was painted in 1506 by Leonardo da Vinci and hangs in the Louvre.

    c. On August 21, 1911, Vincenzo Perruggia stole the Mona Lisa from the Louvre.

    The Louvre was closed to the public on that particular day, and Perruggia, a Louvre employee, simply cut the famous painting from its frame and walked out of the museum. He took it to his home in Paris and hid it in a trunk for two years. In 1913, Perruggia tried to sell the painting to Italy, his native country, for $95,000. He was immediately arrested by Italian officials. The Mona Lisa was returned unharmed to France.

## BEING PRECISE

When you write an objective report, it is necessary to be *precise*. You must give *exact* details—exact times, names, places, and numbers. For example, when writing a report about an automobile accident, you should not say, "A few pedestrians were injured," but rather, "Four pedestrians were injured." When you are reporting on a fire, it is more exact to write "The fire started at 9:00 A.M." than "The fire occurred in the morning."

### Exercise 4C

Each of the following sentences contains some imprecise information. Underline this imprecise information. Then rewrite each sentence to make it more exact.

1.    The winner of the Great Race was a woman.

*The winner of the Great Race was Maria Gonzales.*

2.    The train accident happened somewhere near Lewistown.

3.    Many people were killed in the crash of Flight 19.

4.    Thomas McBain was arrested near his home.

5.    Some fire fighters were overcome by smoke.

6.    Vesna Moore lost control of her car and hit someone.

7.    The final World Series baseball game took place sometime last week.

## GRAMMAR AND PUNCTUATION

### Punctuation with Introductory Phrases

Several sentences in Composition 4 begin with introductory phrases. A **phrase** is a grammatical unit of two or more words without a verb. When a phrase occurs before the main clause, it is called an **introductory phrase.** An introductory phrase, like an introductory clause, is usually followed by a comma. The comma usually separates the introductory phrase from the subject of the sentence. Notice that when the phrase is at the end of the sentence, it requires no punctuation.

#### EXAMPLES

*At Lincoln Avenue*, she turned left.

*Moments later*, the police arrived.

　　　　　BUT

She turned left *at Lincoln Avenue.*

The police arrived *moments later.*

### Exercise 4D

Underline all the examples of introductory phrases in the report on page 35.

### Exercise 4E

Decide if the following sentences begin with introductory phrases. If so, put commas where necessary.

1.　Near the post office, John Slovak lost control of his automobile.

2.　At the age of twenty-six Albert Einstein published his theory of relativity.

3.　The police arrived at the scene of the accident moments after it happened.

4.　Color television was first introduced in the U.S. in 1951.

5.　In the town of Belleview the express train ran off the track.

6.　At the end of World War II representatives from fifty nations helped write the United Nations charter.

7.　It was snowing hard when he hit the parked car.

8.　Right in front of her home on Elm Avenue Jeannette Lupis slipped on the ice and broke her leg.

9.　From 1920 to 1933 James Joyce's *Ulysses* was banned in the U.S.

10.　At the corner of Forbes Avenue and Waverly Drive the crowded bus hit a telephone pole.

11.　Every four years athletes from around the world meet and compete in the Olympic Games.

12.　The construction of the Taj Mahal started in 1632 and was finished twenty years later.

## Punctuation with Appositives

A noun or a noun phrase that immediately follows another noun is called an appositive. An appositive explains or defines the noun it follows and is generally set off by commas. Below are examples from the composition on page 35.

### EXAMPLES

Mary Chan, *town council member*, had an automobile accident.

(Mary Chan = town council member)

She was driving down Main Street with a passenger, *Jane Fields*.

(passenger = Jane Fields)

The driver of the other car, *Joseph Schwartz*, told police that his neck hurt.

(the driver of the other car = Joseph Schwartz)

### Exercise 4F

Decide if these sentences contain appositives. If so, underline the appositives and set them off with commas.

1.  The pedestrian, Ivan Popovich, was not seriously injured.

2.  The vaccine for rabies was discovered in 1885 by Louis Pasteur a French scientist.

3.  The car a 1979 Toyota was badly damaged.

4.  Route 401 a major highway through Clayton was very icy last Friday night.

5.  The fire at 313 Sheradon Drive caused a great deal of damage.

6.  Margaret Mead the famous anthropologist died in 1979 at the age of eighty.

7.  Sarah Lloyd's father a passenger in the taxi was not injured in the accident.

8.  An explosion occurred in the chemical factory in Millvale.

9.  The truck avoided hitting the parked car a 1980 Ford.

10. Abraham Lincoln the sixteenth president of the United States is a national hero.

11. Atari a toy and game manufacturer came out with Pong the first video game in 1972.

12. On Venus the closest planet to the earth there is no water and thus no life.

13. The riot started in a small town called Perth.

14. William Roentgen the discoverer of X rays received the Nobel Prize in physics in 1901.

15. The Library of Congress in Washington is the largest library in the world.

## Indirect Speech

When we wish to report what someone else has said, we often change the speaker's exact words from **direct speech** to **indirect speech.** Indirect speech is frequently used in reports.

When changing from direct to indirect speech

- use the **past tense** of the verb if the statement was originally made in the **present tense**

- (optional) insert *that* when reporting a statement

- change pronouns where necessary

- drop the quotation marks

### EXAMPLES

Direct Speech:      Ali Luzeri said, "I *feel* fine."
Indirect Speech:   Ali Luzeri reported (that) he *felt* fine.

Direct Speech:      Leslie Hoffman said, "I *think* my car *is* badly damaged."
Indirect Speech:   Leslie Hoffman said (that) she *thought* her car *was* badly damaged.

Direct Speech:      The police officer told the woman, "I *want* to see your license."
Indirect Speech:   The police officer told the woman (that) he *wanted* to see her license.

The following verbs are used to introduce reported statements: *tell, say, report,* and *announce. Report* and *announce* are used when something is said formally, such as in a newspaper or at a formal gathering. Notice that *tell* must always be followed by an **indirect object:**

She told *someone* that . . .

She said that . . .

He reported that . . .

He announced that . . .

## Exercise 4G

The following statements were made at the scene of an automobile accident. Change all the statements to indirect speech.

*The driver at fault, Mr. Manning, said that the road was very slippery.*

*Mrs. Manning, a passenger, told a reporter that she wasn't injured.*

# Student Plan 4
## Rain Causes Accident

Imagine that you are a reporter for the school newspaper. A fellow student, Jim Parks, had an accident near school, and you are reporting it. Use the following pictures to guide you in making notes for the report. Make your information detailed and precise. Add more details if you wish. Work with a partner.

### Helpful vocabulary:

skid on wet pavement        knock over

sidewalk        dented (car or motorcycle)

pedestrians

*Main idea sentence\** _____

_____

_____

_____

\*You may want to write your main idea sentence after you finish the plan.

# Student Composition 4
## *Rain Causes Accident*

### Stepping Along

**Step 1:** Write a one-paragraph report using your main idea sentence, your plan, at least one introductory phrase, and appositives to identify each person who was involved in the accident. Be precise.

**Step 2:** Exchange compositions with a partner. As you read your partner's report, think about these questions.

- Do you get a clear picture of the accident from this report?

- Has your partner included all important details?

- Can you give your partner any suggestions for improvement?

**Step 3:** Talk with your partner about your compositions and try to agree on improvements you can make.

**Step 4:** Rewrite your composition, making any changes you feel are necessary.

**Further steps:** As directed by your instructor.

# 5

## *The First Manned Flight to the Moon*

## PLANNING

A student was asked by his history teacher to write a brief report about the first flight to the moon. He went to the library, looked in old newspapers, and took these notes. He forgot to write important information about July 21. *Can you add it?* (Look at the pictures.)

> **JULY 16**
>
> 9:32 A.M. —Apollo 11 blasted off from Cape Kennedy (with Armstrong, Aldrin + Collins)
>
> **JULY 20**
>
> —Armstrong + Aldrin moved from the command module (Columbia) into the lunar module (Eagle)
> — The Eagle descended toward the moon
>
> 4:18 P.M. — They landed (in the Sea of Tranquility)
> — Total time there: 21 hrs. + 37 mins.

## WRITING

The student's final draft looked like this. How is it different from his notes?

> ### The First Manned Flight to the Moon
>
> The first manned flight to the moon began when Apollo 11 blasted off from Cape Kennedy, Florida, at 9:32 A.M. on July 16, 1969, with Armstrong, Aldrin, and Collins as the astronauts. Four days after the blast-off, Armstrong and Aldrin moved from the command module, Columbia, into the lunar module, Eagle, and the two modules separated. Collins continued to orbit the moon in the command module, while the other astronauts descended toward the moon. At 4:18 P.M. on July 20, the Eagle landed on the moon in the Sea of Tranquility. The two astronauts spent twenty-one hours and thirty-seven minutes on the moon. They started back to earth at 1:55 P.M. on July 21.

# ORGANIZATION

### Exercise 5A   Being Precise

The following report contains some imprecise information. Read it and underline the information that could be more exact. Then rewrite the report below, making the imprecise date more exact.

> Sometime last week, Stephen Wosko hijacked a Pacific Southwest 727 in a city in California. He held some crew members hostage for several hours until he finally surrendered to the FBI. Before he surrendered, he read a statement saying that he had hijacked the plane in order to protest the government's recent foreign policy statements.

*Rewritten Paragraph*

_____

_____

_____

_____

_____

_____

_____

_____

_____

_____

_____

_____

## Exercise 5B    Irrelevant Sentences

Read the following reports. Find the sentence in each paragraph that does not support the main idea sentence. Cross it out.

1.      On the night of April 14, 1912, during its first trip from England to New York City, the *Titanic* struck an iceberg in the North Atlantic Ocean and sank. The North Atlantic is now patrolled by the Coast Guard. The tragedy occurred about 1,600 miles (2,560 kilometers) northeast of New York City. The 66,000-ton (60,060 metric tons) ship was carrying 1,316 passengers and a crew of 891. There were not enough lifeboats for everybody, and hundreds of people jumped into the icy waters. No one knows exactly how many people died.

2.      At 7:30 A.M. on March 28, 1979, there was a report of a severe accident in the No. 2 reactor at the Three Mile Island nuclear power plant near Middletown, Pennsylvania. Radioactive gases were escaping through the plant's venting system, and there was a large hydrogen bubble in the top of the reactor. Nuclear experts announced the possibility of an explosion. On March 30, Pennsylvania's governor, Richard Thornburgh, closed twenty-three schools in the area and ordered pregnant women and preschool children to leave the area. Radiation produced by X rays is also dangerous to unborn babies. The crisis lasted thirteen days.

3.      On May 18, 1980, Mount St. Helens erupted violently. The volcano sent hot mud, ash, and gases down its sides. Thick ash clouds rose 12 miles (19.2 kilometers) above the earth and turned day into night over a large area of the state of Washington. The explosion leveled 25,000 acres (10,000 hectares) of timber, destroyed dozens of homes, and washed out numerous bridges and roads. The damage was estimated at almost one billion dollars. At least 32 people died in the disaster. In 1979, the eruption of Mt. Simila in the Batur district of central Java killed 175 people.

# GRAMMAR AND PUNCTUATION

## Additional Uses of the Comma

In addition to the uses of the comma that you have already learned, commas are used with dates, with names of places, and with numerals to separate thousands.

### Dates

Use a comma to separate a day from a month:

Wednesday, July 16     Sunday, May 4

Use a comma to separate a date from a year:

June 13, 1990     May 1, 1952

Use a comma after a year that follows a date:

July 16, 1969, was the date of the *Apollo 11* lift-off.

My sister got married on July 8, 1960, in Baltimore.

*Don't* use a comma between a month and a year:

November 1975     February 1950

### Place Names

Use a comma to separate a city from a state or a city from a country:

Houston, Texas     Paris, France

Use a comma after a state that follows a city:

Cleveland, Ohio, is my hometown.

### Numerals

Use a comma with numerals to separate thousands:

10,000     77,850     244,930

Exercise 5C

Put a comma where necessary in the following sentences. Some sentences include uses of the comma that you learned earlier.

1. On April 30 1978 Naomi Uemura became the first man to reach the North Pole alone by dogsled.

2. John Kennedy thirty-fifth president of the United States was born on May 29 1917 in Brookline Massachusetts.

3. On April 18 1979 the United States Senate voted to turn over the Panama Canal to Panama by a vote of 68 to 32.

4. The United States Japan and forty-seven other nations signed the Japanese peace treaty in San Francisco California on September 8 1951.

5. An overcrowded bus fell into Lake Victoria on July 14 1979.

6. In Youngstown Ohio four hundred municipal employees walked off their jobs on Wednesday April 6.

7. Over 65000 people marched in Washington on May 6 1979 to protest the use of nuclear power.

8. On November 19 1978 more than 900 followers of the People's Temple cult died in the Guyana jungle after drinking poisoned Kool-Aid.

9. In 1988 Soviet Armenia experienced one of the worst earthquakes in the history of the U.S.S.R.

10. After the elevator was invented in the 1860s city buildings began to be built higher than five stories.

## Indirect Speech

You already learned that when you indirectly report a statement made in the *present* tense, you must change it to the *past* tense. Similarly, when you report a statement made in the **present continuous tense,** you must change it to the **past continuous tense.** Remember that a present continuous verb is formed with *am/is/are* + verb + *ing* (I *am listening,* she *is studying,* they *are sleeping*). A past continuous verb is formed with *was/were* + verb + *ing* (I *was listening,* she *was studying,* they *were sleeping*).

### EXAMPLES

Direct Speech:     Pedro said, "I *am studying* chemical engineering."
Indirect Speech:   Pedro said (that) he *was studying* chemical engineering.

Direct Speech:     Mira told me, "I *am doing* a report in my writing class."
Indirect Speech:   Mira told me (that) she *was doing* a report in her writing class.

## Exercise 5D

Change the following statements to indirect speech, using all the information in parentheses. Notice that some of the statements are in the present continuous tense while others are in the simple present tense. Use *said, told* or *announced,* as appropriate, to introduce the reported statements.

1.     "We're flying over the Atlantic Ocean."
       (an hour after takeoff, the stewardess ⟶ the passengers)

       *An hour after takeoff, the stewardess told the passengers that they were flying over the Atlantic Ocean.*

2.     "When I want to read a novel, I write one."
       (Benjamin Disraeli, one of Britian's most distinguished prime ministers)

       *Benjamin Disraeli, one of Britain's most distinguished prime ministers, said that when he wanted to read a novel, he wrote one.*

3. "I'm an introvert in an extrovert profession."
   (during his presidency, Richard Nixon ⟶ friends)

4. "When I am working on a book or a story, I write every morning as soon after first light as possible."
   (Ernest Hemingway)

5. "I belong to the gods."
   (Isadora Duncan, a famous dancer)

6. "I have nothing to declare except my genius."
   (in 1882, Oscar Wilde, English playwright ⟶ New York customs officials)

7.    "I am embarking on a wide ocean..."
      (in 1775, shortly after his election, George Washington ⟶ an audience)

8.    "I am the greatest."
      (at the height of his boxing career, Muhammad Ali)

9.    "I want to bind up the nation's wounds."
      (after the Civil War, Abraham Lincoln ⟶ fellow Americans)

10.   "I am reading the press more and enjoying it less."
      (during his presidency, John Kennedy)

# Student Plan 5
## A Historic Event

A. Write some notes for a brief report about a historic event that interests you.

OR

B. Prepare to write about Charles Lindbergh's historic flight across the Atlantic Ocean. It was the first nonstop solo transatlantic flight.

With a partner or a small group, discuss the pictures. Can you add ideas of your own? Use these pictures and your own ideas to write some notes. Use the first picture for your main idea sentence. Make your information detailed and precise.

### Helpful vocabulary:

| | |
|---|---|
| takeoff (n), take off (v) | land at |
| pilot | greet   saludar (presentarse a) |
| parachute | medal |
| radio | national hero |
| fly over (countries) | symbol of aviation |
| in _____ hours | |

*Main idea sentence*  _____

_____

_____

_____

_____

_____

*Use the first picture to help you write your main idea sentence.

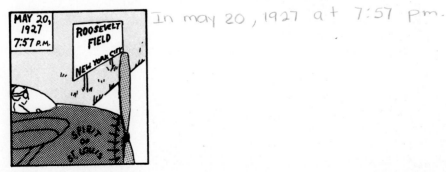

In may 20, 1927 at 7:57 pm.

Note: The X on the pictures shows that Lindbergh did not have these items in his plane.

# *Student Composition 5*
## *A Historic Event*

### Stepping Along

**Step 1:** Use your main idea sentence and plan to help you write a one-paragraph report. Be precise, and use correct punctuation.

**Step 2:** Exchange compositions with a partner. As you read your partner's report, think about these questions.

- Is everything in this report clear to you?

- Has your partner included all important details?

- Is the punctuation correct?

- Can you give your partner any suggestions for improvement?

**Step 3:** Talk with your partner about your reports. Try to agree on improvements you can make.

**Step 4:** Rewrite your composition, making any changes you feel are necessary.

**Further steps:** As directed by your instructor.

# 6
# *Independence Day in Middleburg*

## PLANNING

A reporter in the small town of Middleburg visited the Fourth of July festivities and took these notes during the day. He didn't write notes on the last three events. *Can you add them?* (Look at the pictures.)

```
July 4 - Middleburg
1. Parade from City Hall (10:45)        5. Mayor awarded
 - Calvin HS Band at head                  prizes
 - Also fire fighters (St 29)           6. Softball game
    Boy Scouts (Troop 240)                 between Calvin H.S.
    majorettes (Seabrook JHS)              and Woodrow H.S.
2. Parade reached                        - Tigers won (7-3)
    Ambrose Park (12:20)
3. Mayor's speech
4. Games & races (2-4)
    Winners
 - Jeffrey Boyd (pie-eating)
 - Wilma Petrov (potato sack)
 - J.+J. Bonney (3-legged race)
```

## WRITING

His report appeared like this the next day. *Underline the main idea sentence. Circle the words and phrases that show time order.*

### INDEPENDENCE DAY IN MIDDLEBURG

On July 4, Middleburg held its annual Independence Day celebration. A parade left City Hall at 10:45 a.m. The Calvin High School band marched at the head of the parade. Fire fighters from Station 29, Boy Scouts from troop 240, and majorettes from Seabrook Junior High School were also among the participants. At 12:20 p.m., the parade reached Ambrose Park, where Mayor Rita Pasquarelli addressed the crowd. After the speech, there were games and races in the park from 2:00 until 4:00 p.m. Jeffrey Boyd won the pie-eating contest. Wilma Petrov won the potato-sack race, and Joan and James Bonney finished first in the three-legged race. Mayor Pasquarelli awarded prizes to the winners. A softball game between Calvin High School and Woodrow High School followed. The team from Woodrow High School, the Tigers, won the game 7 to 3. At 6:30 p.m., the picnic started. Afterward, from 7:30 to 9:30, the band played dance music. The celebration ended with a fireworks display.

# ORGANIZATION

## Major Points and Additional Details

As you have learned, a main idea sentence must be followed by major points. As your compositions become longer and more developed, the major points will be followed by additional details. These details give additional information about the major points. Additional details will make your composition more interesting and more complete.

In a report, the major points are the events. In a longer report, **additional details** about the events can be included. Here is an example from the newspaper report of a major point followed by additional details.

### EXAMPLE

| Major point: | A parade left City Hall at 10:45 A.M. |
|---|---|
| Additional details: | The Calvin High School Band marched at the head of the parade. |
| | Fire fighters from Station 29, Boy Scouts from troop 240, and majorettes from Seabrook Junior High School were among the participants. |

The major point mentions an event (the parade). The next two statements give details about it—they tell specific things about the parade.

Now read the newspaper report again. Find the statements that give additional details about events.

## Exercise 6A

In the following reports, underline each major point twice. Underline each statement that gives additional detail once. The first sentence in each report is the main idea sentence.

1.    The Royal Oak Art Festival took place last week. <u>The festival began at 9:30 A.M. on August 9 with a speech by the director of the Artists' Guild, Meredith Ainsley.</u> <u>She welcomed everyone to the ninth annual festival.</u> There was entertainment on the stage for the next hour. First, the Polish Folk Organization presented some traditional dances. After that, a group of children from Oakmont Elementary School gave a short play. At 10:30, local artists opened their booths and began a program of craft demonstrations. Ronald Taylor, a local glassblower, demonstrated the art of glassblowing. Viola Eggars, a weaver, demonstrated the use of the loom. At noon, the food booths opened and many types of ethnic food were sold. The Greek booth sold lamb shish kebab, spinach pie, and baklava. The Japanese booth sold sushi and sukiyaki, and the Polish booth sold stuffed cabbage. The festival closed at 8:00 P.M.

2.      On August 30, 1979, Hurricane David began a week of destruction in the Caribbean and in parts of the U.S. The savage storm ripped across the islands of Dominica and Puerto Rico on August 30. Scores of people were left dead, injured, or homeless. On August 31, the hurricane headed north and struck the Dominican Republic. More than 1,000 people were killed, and thousands were injured. The 100-miles-per-hour winds and huge tides destroyed crops, power lines, and water supplies. In addition, an estimated 100,000 people lost their homes. On September 3, Hurricane David hit Florida near Palm Beach. Power lines were knocked out, and buildings and cars suffered heavy damage. The following day, the storm headed inland, across the islands off the coast of Georgia. It reached the Northeast on September 7. The storm ripped power lines throughout the area and cut off electricity for more than 2.5 million people in New York. Eight deaths were reported.

Exercise 6B

Read through each short report; then write an appropriate main idea sentence.

1.  _____

    _____

    _____

    _____

The three prisoners captured the sheriff when he brought in a new prisoner. Jail officials then cut off the water supply, and the prisoners in turn threatened to kill the sheriff. On October 16, two days after the prisoners had seized the sheriff, they surrendered. Sheriff Olivetti was unharmed. Officials at the Kent County Jail say the prisoners must stand trial.

2.  _____

    _____

    _____

    _____

The mayor gave a campaign speech at the Lone Pine Motel early last evening. After the speech, he left the motel. Mayor Crosby returned about 2:00 A.M. Witnesses say he then banged loudly on the door of Harold Ruiz's room. When Ruiz opened the door, the mayor pulled out a gun and shot him. He immediately surrendered to authorities, claiming Ruiz had been blackmailing him.

3.  _____

    _____

    _____

    _____

Beame, a maintenance worker for the Skyway Building, was washing the second-floor windows early Tuesday morning when he lost his balance and tumbled to the ground. Witnesses called an ambulance, and Beame was rushed to Montgomery County Hospital. Emergency room personnel announced that both his legs were paralyzed. Doctors now say that he will regain the use of his legs.

# GRAMMAR AND PUNCTUATION

## Capitalization

Capitalization is often required in English. Here are some examples of words or phrases that are capitalized.

**First words of sentences:**

*Several students jogged through the park.*

**Names of people:**

*Marie Curie, Karl Marx*

**Specific places and locations:**

*Central Park, New York, United States*

**Streets:**

*Fifth Avenue, Scott Street*

**Schools:**

*Boston University, Lake Taylor High School*

**Nationalities:**

*American, Venezuelan*

**Languages:**

*Arabic, Japanese*

**Song titles:**

*"The Star-Spangled Banner," "Yesterday"*

**Book titles:**

*For Whom the Bell Tolls, Animal Farm*

**Holidays:**

*Thanksgiving, Valentine's Day*

**Organizations:**

*United Nations, Pittsburgh Steelers*

**Days of the week and months:**

*Tuesday, Saturday, June, August*

**Names and titles of people:**

*President Kennedy, Professor Steinmann, Ms. Whitehurst*

Exercise 6C

Circle the letters that need to be capitalized in the following paragraphs.

1.

arlington national cemetery in arlington, virginia, contains the remains of many important americans. president john fitzgerald kennedy was buried there on november 25, 1963. the remains of his brother, senator robert f. kennedy, were laid to rest near him on june 8, 1968. soldiers from every war are also buried in arlington cemetery. on november 11, 1921, an unknown soldier from the first world war was interred there, and on memorial day, may 30, 1958, two unidentified soldiers from later wars were buried near him.

2.

on may 28, lisa johns graduated from eastern michigan university in ypsilanti, michigan. she is the daughter of mr. and mrs. harold johns of frankstown road in pittsburgh. ms. johns majored in music and wrote an original song, "late night blues," for her senior project. she plans to spend the summer traveling in france.

3.

the famous pop group known as the beatles first played together in liverpool, england, in 1961. they made thirteen albums and three movies and greatly influenced a generation of young people. on august 26, 1966, the beatles gave their last concert at candlestick park in san francisco. the group recorded its last album, *let it be*, in 1970.

### Exercise 6D    Review of Punctuation

Punctuate the following sentences correctly. Be prepared to explain why you used the punctuation as you did.

1. Rudolph Diesel a German engineer invented the diesel engine in 1895.

2. Before you wax your car make sure it is completely dry.

3. The four most common names in the United States are Smith Johnson Williams and Brown.

4. At the corner of Wood and Fifth a truck hit a Greyhound bus.

5. On August 21 1959 Hawaii was admitted to the U.S. as its fiftieth state.

6. Check your arrival and departure dates carefully before you make your reservations.

7. Remove the cake from the pan when it is done and place it on a rack to cool.

8. America's first earth-orbiting space station *Skylab* crashed down in the Indian Ocean and on parts of Australia on July 11 1979.

9. After you loosen the dirt in your garden with a hoe use a rake to remove the rocks and weeds.

10. Caviar a delicacy of fish eggs is produced only in Russia Iran and Romania.

11. In 1895 twenty-one-year-old Guglielmo Marconi made the world's first radio in Bologna Italy.

12. Be sure to tip the waiter before you leave the restaurant.

# Student Plan and Composition 6

Develop your own topic, or choose one of the topics below for a final report. You will be writing to inform your classmates about an event. Imagine that you are writing this report for your school newspaper. Think like a reporter.

1. Tell what occurred at a specific holiday (or wedding) celebration in your country.

2. Report on a significant historical event (political, social, or scientific) that took place in your country.

3. Tell what happened at an accident (automobile, fire, and so on) that you recently witnessed.

4. *MORE CHALLENGING:* Think of a recent news event that interests you. It may be of local, national, or international importance (perhaps a sports event, a space journey, a crime, an accident, a political meeting, a birth, a death, and so on). Read about it in newspapers and newsmagazines and/or listen to TV or radio news. Take notes about the event, and *in your own words*, explain what happened.

## Stepping Along

**Step 1:** After choosing your topic, take time to think and write chronological notes.

**Step 2:** Form groups of about three students. Take turns reading your notes to one another. Stop one another and ask questions when you think a point is missing or when something is not clear. Tell one another where you are interested in knowing additional details.

**Step 3:** Use your notes and your partners' suggestions to write your report. Consider your partners as your *audience*.

**Step 4:** When you finish writing, get into the same group of three students. Read both of your partners' reports. As you read each report, think about these questions.

- Would you like to know more details about any part of the report?

- Is there any part of the report that is not completely clear to you?

- Could this report be used in your school newspaper as it is written?

- Can you give your partner suggestions for improvement?

**Step 5:** Talk with your partners about these questions. Try to agree on improvements that you can make.

**Step 6:** Rewrite your composition, making any changes you feel are necessary.

**Further steps:** As directed by your instructor.

# Unit 3

## Analyzing by Cause and Effect

In this unit, you will learn to look at an event or situation (effect) and examine the reasons or causes behind it. You analyze the cause of a situation when you wonder why your new shirt shrank or why you received a bad grade in a course. Sometimes there is only one obvious cause for an effect. For example, your 100-percent cotton shirt shrank because you washed it in hot water. Frequently, however, there is more than one probable cause of a situation, and it is important to examine all causes. Perhaps you received a bad grade in a course because you were absent too many times, got a D on your term paper, and failed your final exam. When you look at *multiple* causes, there is often one cause that is the most important. If your final exam counted for 75 percent of your final grade, that was the main reason you got a bad grade in your course.

When you write about the reasons for a situation, remember the following things.

1. *Examine all the causes.* If an event or situation has more than one cause, discuss all of them. If the economy of a country is failing, for example, there are probably several reasons.

2. *Support all the causes.* Give good examples to support each cause. For example, if one reason for a government's unpopularity is that it has passed certain laws, you need to give at least one example of these laws.

3. *Save your most important cause for last.* This makes your paper more interesting and gives it a strong conclusion. Also, if you put the most important cause first, your reader may feel it is not necessary to continue reading.

4. *Don't make judgments.* Be objective. A cause-effect composition doesn't recommend how to change the situation or give opinions about why the situation is good or bad. It simply examines the reasons for it.

People in all fields make use of this kind of organization when they write. A political science student, for example, might be asked to explain why a government fell. An ecologist might need to analyze why a particular lake or stream is polluted. Or a civil engineer might have to examine the reasons for the collapse of a certain bridge. In all of these cases, the purpose for writing is the same: to explain *why*.

**67**

# 7
## *Why Blake College Is Popular*

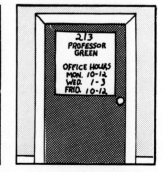

## PLANNING

The recruitment officer of Blake College is putting together a pamphlet to send to high-school students in the area. She wants to explain why Blake College is so popular. Before writing, she made a list of the causes (reasons). She also included some details to support her reasons.

```
1. Beautiful campus       3. Extracurricular activities
   - trees                   - films
   - grass                   - lectures
   - handsome buildings      - dances
                             - concerts
2. Good facilities        4. Affordable tuition - $900/sem.
   - new gym
   - computer labs        5. Outstanding faculty
   - large library           - interesting classes
                             - helpful professors
```

## WRITING

The article appeared like this in the pamphlet. How is it different from her plan?

Calendar

August 10 — Orientation

September 14 — Classes Begin

October 12 — Homecoming

### WELCOME TO BLAKE COLLEGE!

Every year more students are seeking admission to Blake College, and there are several reasons for our popularity. First of all, our campus is beautiful. We have trees, acres of grass, and handsome, well-kept buildings. In addition, the college has excellent facilities, such as a new gymnasium, computer labs, and a large library. On weekends, there are always plenty of extracurricular activities to choose from, such as films, lectures, dances, and concerts. The tuition, moreover, is an affordable $900 per semester. But the major reason for the success of Blake College is our outstanding faculty. Classes are interesting and informative and our professors are always ready to give individualized help.

# ORGANIZATION

## Understanding the Cause-Effect Relationship

In this unit, you will learn to explain the cause or causes of an effect. The following examples show the cause-effect relationship. Notice that an effect can have more than one cause.

### EXAMPLES

He feels tired today.     (effect)
Why?
He did not sleep well last night.     (cause)

My car will not start.     (effect)
Why?
I left the car lights on all night.     (cause)

The police are on strike.     (effect)
Why?
They want a salary increase.     (cause)
They want additional health benefits.     (cause)
They want more vacation time.     (cause)

## Exercise 7A

Decide which statement is the *cause* and which is the *effect*.

1. _____*cause*_____ → The roads were icy.

   _____*effect*_____ → There were many accidents.

2. _____*effect*_____ Jim stopped smoking cigarettes.

   _____*cause*_____ The price of cigarettes went up.

3. _____*cause*_____ The experiment succeeded.

   _____*effect*_____ The experiment was conducted carefully.

4. _____ Lucy is happy.

   _____ Lucy won the lottery.

5. _____ There was a severe storm last night.

   _____ Many buildings were damaged.

6. _____ The plants were not watered for a month.

   _____ The plants died.

Exercise 7B

For each of the following situations, read the accompanying statements carefully. Circle the statement or statements that are possible causes of the situation.

1.   The Eberlee pharmacy is a very successful business operation.

    **a.** The clerks are friendly and helpful.

    **b.** The merchandise is reasonably priced.

    **c.** The owners work hard.

2.   The majority of students failed the history test that Professor Dunn gave yesterday.

    **a.** The test was difficult.

    **b.** The students didn't study.

    **c.** Many students are enrolled in Professor Dunn's class.

3.   The Lima City Council decided to cancel its August meeting.

    **a.** The city council has thirty active members.

    **b.** Many of the council members take a vacation in August.

    **c.** Each monthly meeting lasts approximately three hours.

4.   The new wing of the Lawrence library, scheduled to be completed in 1988, was not completed until 1990.

    **a.** The construction workers were on strike for nearly a year.

    **b.** The library was noisy during the period of construction.

    **c.** The bricks needed for construction were delivered eight months late.

5.   Flight #54 from Los Angeles to Chicago was postponed for two hours.

    **a.** Los Angeles has a very large airport.

    **b.** The pilot of the plane became ill.

    **c.** The plane seats 200 people.

## Major Points and Additional Details

Remember that when you write, you must support your main idea sentence with **major points.** When you analyze the cause of a situation, your main idea sentence will tell the situation or **effect,** and your major points will tell the **causes.** In the plan of the composition, 1, 2, 3, 4, and 5 are the major points. These major points are repeated below.

*1. Beautiful campus*
*2. Good facilities*
*3. Extracurricular activities*
*4. Affordable tuition*
*5. Outstanding faculty*

However, if the composition included only the above major points, it would sound incomplete. A good cause-effect composition needs additional details. Look back at the plan of the composition on page 69. Notice how additional details are added to each major point. Sometimes additional details follow in the next sentence. Sometimes they are included in the same sentence with the major point.

### Exercise 7C

Read the following cause-effect paragraphs. Underline twice each major point. Underline once the sentences that give additional details. The first sentence of each paragraph is the main idea sentence.

1. There are four major reasons I like New York City. First of all, I think it is a beautiful city. It is filled with sleek glass skyscrapers; charming, old stone buildings; and attractive parks and squares. Second, I enjoy the cultural life that New York offers. Exciting concerts, Broadway plays, and new films are always available, as are museum exhibitions from all over the world. In addition, I appreciate the light entertainment the city offers. Nowhere else in the United States can one find so many delightful restaurants, nightclubs, cabarets, and discotheques. Finally, I like the diversity of people in New York City. The city has the largest tourist population in the world. It also has colorful ethnic neighborhoods such as Little Italy, Harlem, Spanish Harlem, and Chinatown.

2. There are a number of known causes of cancer. Excessive exposure to radiation is one of the most common causes of skin cancer. The sun's rays contain radiation. So do X rays. Exposure to toxic substances is another of the many causes of this disease. Asbestos, for example, is associated with lung cancer, and vinyl chloride has been linked to liver cancer. Smoking is probably the most well-known cause. Smoking cigarettes, cigars, and pipes is responsible for lip, throat, and lung cancer.

Exercise 7D

Below, plans of the preceding paragraphs have been started. Complete the plans, showing both the major points and the additional details.

1.  *Main idea sentence:* There are four major reasons I like New York City.

    *1. Beautiful city*
    *— glass skyscrapers*
    *— old stone buildings*
    *— parks and squares*

2.  *Main idea sentence:* There are a number of known causes of cancer.

    *1. Exposure to radiation*
    *— sun's rays*

## Main Idea Sentences

A main idea sentence for a cause-effect composition usually tells the reader (1) what the event or situation is and (2) that there are causes or reasons for the situation. The number of causes is also mentioned (such as *several reasons, two major causes, three important reasons*).

### EXAMPLES

```
 ┌───── effect ──────────────┐┌─── causes ────────┐
```
Accidents involving aircraft occur for a variety of reasons.

```
 ┌──── causes ──────┐┌──── effect ─────────┐
```
There are three causes for her lack of success in the course.

### Exercise 7E

Read the following cause-effect paragraphs carefully. Then circle the best main idea sentence for each.

1.    **a.** The poor attendance in Professor O'Toole's class has several causes.

      **b.** There are several reasons the classroom is uncomfortable.

      **c.** Students do not attend Professor O'Toole's class.

   First, the classroom is uncomfortable. It is very warm, and there are no windows for ventilation. In addition, the class meets at 8:00 A.M. This hour is too early for most college students. Most important of all, students seldom attend this class because of the teacher. He is an unpleasant, humorless man, and his lectures are boring.

2.    **a.** Americans should get more exercise and eat better food.

      **b.** A large percentage of Americans are overweight for two major reasons.

      **c.** Americans should drive less for two major reasons.

   First, because of automation, many Americans get little or no exercise. The automobile, especially, is to blame. Driving is faster and easier than walking but does not keep the body trim. In addition, the diet of many Americans is responsible for obesity. Such fattening foods as hamburgers, French fries, cakes, and cookies are common foods in the American diet.

3.    **a.** Americans are moving for several reasons.

   **b.** Americans do not like snow for several reasons.

   **c.** There are several reasons many Americans are moving from northern states to southwestern states such as Texas and Arizona.

First of all, Americans are moving to escape the cold and the snow of the North. The Southwest offers warmth and sun almost year-round, and this gentle climate allows people to be much more active outdoors. Furthermore, because of the warm climate, the cost of heating a home in the Southwest is much less than in the North, and many Americans move to save heating costs. And finally, many Americans are tired of the crowds and the stress in the northern cities. They relocate in the Southwest hoping to find freedom and peace in its wide-open spaces.

## Transitions Showing Addition

When you are listing causes or other ideas in a composition, you should use transitions that show addition to introduce your major points. The following transitions are appropriate for a composition that lists several causes for an event. Notice the punctuation used with each.

First (of all), . . .

Another reason is . . .

In addition, . . .

Also, . . .

Moreover, . . . also— in addition.

The major (most important) reason is . . . /Finally, . . .

*In addition* and *moreover* do not always appear at the beginning of the sentence. Note the following examples.

**EXAMPLES**

*In addition*, the college has excellent facilities.
The college, *in addition*, has excellent facilities.

*Moreover*, the tuition is expensive.
The tuition, *moreover*, is expensive.

## Exercise 7F

Underline the transitions used in Composition 7.

### Exercise 7G

The following cause-effect paragraph is poorly written because it lacks transitions. It would be much easier to understand if transitions were used between its major points. Decide where each major supporting statement begins, and insert appropriate transitions. Rewrite the paragraph in the space provided below.

> There are three reasons Mr. Tucker was fired from his job. He was often absent from work. He missed thirty working days last year. His personality was a problem. He was nasty to other employees and to the customers. His performance on the job was poor. He did not follow the boss's instructions, and he rarely completed assignments.

*Rewritten paragraph*

There are three reasons Mr. Tucker was
fired from his job. First of all, He was
often absent from work. Another reason is,
His personality was a problem. Finally, His
performance on the job was poor.

Exercise 7H

Now do the same with this paragraph.

> Superfair is the most popular supermarket in town for several reasons. The store has a large selection of items. You can find any food you want, even the rarest spice or the most exotic fruit. The prices are very reasonable. A gallon of milk costs no more here than in any other supermarket. Meat costs even less! There are no long waiting lines at the checkout counter. Checkout time is usually no more than five minutes.

*Rewritten paragraph*

_____

_____

_____

_____

_____

_____

_____

_____

_____

_____

_____

_____

_____

# Student Plan 7
## *Why Croft College Is Unpopular*

Imagine that an overseas friend of yours is considering applying to Croft College, a college that you know is very unpopular. You must try to explain to your friend why it is a poor choice. These pictures show you five major reasons for the college's unpopularity. Write a plan and a main idea sentence. Add at least one additional detail to each of your five major points. Use the plan of Composition 7 as a guide.

**Helpful vocabulary:**

trash/garbage          expensive (tuition)

cracked (concrete)     boring (classes)

run-down (buildings)   unhelpful (teachers)

outdated (books)

*Main idea sentence*\* _____

_____

_____

_____

- run down building

- garbage

- unsafe

_____

\*You may want to write your main idea sentence after you finish the plan.

facilities

— library - not many books

— gym - small

78

not enough
extracurricular
activities
-ad films
- no concerts

- tuition is
expensive $500
fall

bad
Faculty
-classes are boring
-no office hour
-unhelpful.

# *Student Composition 7*
## *Why Croft College Is Unpopular*

### Stepping Along

**Step 1:** Use your main idea sentence and your plan and write a one-paragraph composition. Use appropriate transitions to introduce each major point.

**Step 2:** Exchange compositions with a partner. With a pencil, lightly underline *twice* each major point in your partner's composition. Underline *once* each additional detail.
- Did your partner use details to support the major points?
- Did your partner use transitions before major points?
- Can you give your partner any suggestions for improvement?

**Step 3:** Talk with your partner about your compositions. Try to agree on improvements that you can make.

**Step 4:** Rewrite your composition, making any changes you feel are necessary.

**Further steps:** As directed by your instructor.

## Why Sandra Miller Is Not Healthy

## PLANNING

A student wants to write about her roommate, Sandra, who is not in very good health. Before writing, she made an **idea map** to generate ideas. In a circle in the middle of the page, she put her main idea. Then she thought of some major reasons. She put these around the main idea and circled each one. She thought of some details, too, and put them in smaller circles next to the reasons they support.

*She didn't complete her map. Can you? Work with a partner, if you wish, and use the pictures on the opposite page.*

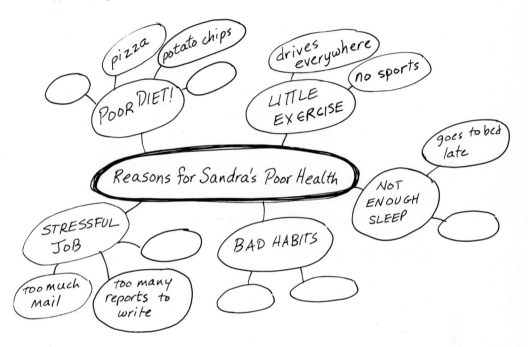

## WRITING

This is the student's final draft. How is it different from the map? *Circle the transition words she uses.*

---

### Why Sandra Miller Is Not Healthy

Several factors might explain my roommate Sandra Miller's poor health. First of all, Sandra seldom eats properly. Her favorite foods are pizza, potato chips, cookies, and candy bars. Second, she gets very little exercise. She drives her car everywhere and prefers watching sports to participating in them. She also seldom gets enough rest. She works late into the night and gets up early. She has, moreover, several bad habits such as excessive smoking and coffee drinking that make her nervous. But the most important cause of Sandra's ill health is probably her job. She feels a great deal of stress and cannot enjoy her work because she has too much to do. She never has enough time to answer all her mail, return all her phone calls, and write all her reports.

## ORGANIZATION

### Exercise 8A    Major Points and Additional Details

Think of the reasons the town or city where you live now is a nice place to live. With a small group or the whole class, make an idea map showing major points and additional details. Add as many new circles as you wish.

## The Cause-Effect Relationship

Many events or situations have more than one cause. Some causes are very important; others are less important. A thorough cause-effect composition, however, considers every cause.

### Exercise 8B

Practice thinking of multiple causes by writing three possible causes for the following effects.

1.     Jack Nolte failed his physics exam.

*He often missed lectures during the semester.*

*He forgot to do a portion of the exam.*

*He had a headache during the exam.*

2.     There are, on the average, over 700,000 fires per year in homes and apartments in the United States.

*not all the houses have smokr alarms*

*The overload the electrical outlets.*

*children play with maches*

3.     Each year, many foreign students come to American colleges and universities to study.

*The test books are up to date.*

*The Libraries are complit.*

*The american degrees has prestiges.*

4.     Some people would rather travel by bus than by plane.

*Because planes are more dangerous than buses*

*Buses are more cheap.*

*They want to enjoy the scenery*

5.     Automobile accidents occur frequently on American highways.

*People don't follow the speed limite.*

*People don't maintain their cars properly*

*wether causes accidents.*

*People drinking drive.*

## Exercise 8C   Irrelevant Sentences

Read the following cause-effect paragraphs. Find a sentence in each paragraph that does not support the main idea sentence. Cross it out.

1.     The Lilac Inn restaurant is losing business for three major reasons. First, customers are staying away because of the unsanitary conditions in the restaurant—the tables are often messy and the floors dirty. In addition, the service is poor. The waiters and waitresses are generally slow and unfriendly. The waiters and waitresses wear uniforms. Most important of all, customers are not pleased with the food at the Lilac Inn. The meals are of poor quality and overpriced.

2.     There are several reasons Henry Ford achieved such success with his automobile. The first reason is that Ford concentrated on making a single model (the Model-T Ford) and was thus able to perfect his product. Moreover, by introducing the assembly-line method to automobile production, he was able to improve production efficiency. Henry Ford also ran for the Senate but lost. Finally, he was successful because of the low price of his cars; in 1921, the cost per car was only $280.

3.     For several reasons, jogging has become a very popular sport in the United States. First of all, in contrast to most other sports, jogging requires no real training. Joggers must only be able to put one foot in front of the other. Occasionally joggers have heart attacks. Americans also like jogging because it is not expensive. The only item they must buy is a pair of good running shoes. Finally, people like the sport because it is easy to observe the progress they are making.

## GRAMMAR AND PUNCTUATION

### Showing Cause-Effect with *Because*

At the sentence level, cause-effect is often expressed by two clauses connected with *because*. *Because* introduces the clause that gives the cause for a situation. This clause can be placed at the beginning or at the end of the sentence. Notice the punctuation in the examples.

### <u>EXAMPLES</u>

Sandra cannot enjoy her job *because* she has too much work.

*Because* she has too much work, Sandra cannot enjoy her job.

### Exercise 8D

Decide first which sentence is the cause and which is the effect. Then combine the sentences with *because*, changing nouns to pronouns where necessary.

1.  DDT is dangerous to animals and humans.
    DDT is now banned in the United States.

    *Because DDT is dangerous to animals and humans, it is now banned in the United States.*

2.  The workers went on strike.
    The workers were unhappy with their wages.

3.  The car will not start.
    The battery is dead.

    *Because the battery is dead, The car will not start*
    *The battery is dead, so the car will not start*
    *The battery is dead; Therefore, the car will not start*

4.  Michigan borders on four of the five Great Lakes.
    Michigan was nicknamed "The Great Lake State."

    *Why does Michigan border on four of the five Great Lake.*
    *Why was michigan nicknamed "The Great Lake State?*

5.  The man robbed a bank.
    The man was sent to prison.

    *(cause)*
    *Why did a man robb a bank.*
    *(topic)*
    *Why was the man sent to prision.*

**Exercise 8E**

Complete the following sentences.

1.    Because Jack needed money, *he got a part-time job washing cars.*

    (topic)
2.    The student passed the test because ___ he studied hard ___ (cause)

    _____ .

3.    Because ___ (cause) the pavement was wet

    ___ (icy) _____ , the car slid. (topic)
    
    slide

4.    We ate a big dinner because ___ we were very hungry ___ .

5.    Because the television set is not plugged in, ___ (cause) the television

    won't turn on .

6.    ___ she didn't go to work

    ___ (she stayed at home) ___ because she felt ill. (c)
    
    happen first (cause)

7.    Because Iris doesn't like to cook, ___ she allways eats

    in restaurants . ( Se didn't volunteer

    to help cook for the party

8.    _____

    ___ They neve get on an ___ because they're afraid to fly. (1) (couse)
    
    airplane

    wh + aux + s + v + c

## Punctuation with Adverbial Clause: Summary

The *because* clause is a dependent adverbial clause that tells *why*. In Unit 1, you studied dependent adverbial clauses that tell *when*—clauses beginning with *before*, *after*, and *when*. These clauses can be placed at the beginning or the end of a sentence. When a clause occurs at the beginning of the sentence, a comma follows it.

### EXAMPLES

*When the omelet becomes firm,* lay thin slices of cheese on it.
Lay thin slices of cheese on the omelet *when it becomes firm.*

*Because she drinks a lot of coffee,* she feels nervous.
She feels nervous *because she drinks a lot of coffee.*

## Exercise 8F

Punctuate these sentences correctly. Some need no additional punctuation.

1.      After you cross the bridge turn right onto Lincoln Road.

2.      In the 1960s many students in the United States participated in marches and demonstrations because they were opposed to the war in Vietnam.

3.      Take the clothes out of the washer when the machine turns off.

4.      Before you do the experiment check the equipment carefully.

5.      Because he could no longer conceal his involvement in the Watergate scandal President Nixon resigned from office in 1974.

6.      Deposit your money before you press the button.

7.      When the American Civil War ended in 1864 the slaves were freed.

8.      After the United States bought Alaska from Russia in 1867 gold and oil were discovered there.

# Student Plan 8
## Why Bob Adams (or Someone You Know) Is Healthy

*(Home work)*

A. Make a map with your ideas about why someone you know is in good health.

OR

B. Imagine that Sandra Miller is a friend of yours, and you want to persuade her to change her lifestyle. You have a mutual friend, Bob Adams, who is in very good health. Explain to Sandra the reasons for Bob's good health.

   With a partner or a small group, discuss the pictures. Together, make an idea map of the reasons for Bob's good health. (Note: There are *five* major points.)

### Helpful vocabulary:

| | |
|---|---|
| well-balanced (meals) | play baseball/tennis |
| vegetables | alcohol |
| fruit | go to bed |
| meat | get up |
| exercise regularly | get along well with (coworkers) |

*Main idea sentence*\* _____

_____

_____

_____

_____

\*You may want to write your main idea sentence after you finish the plan.


**YOUR IDEA MAP**

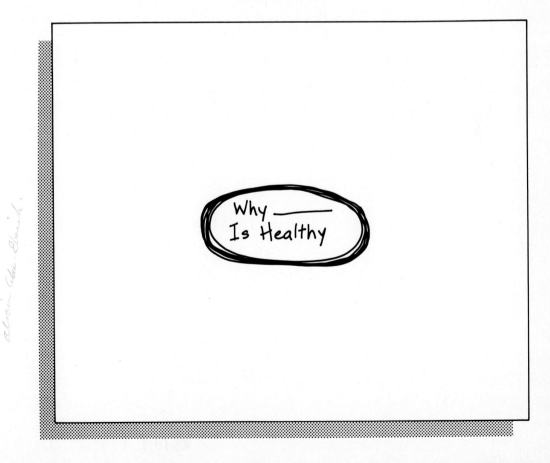

# Student Composition 8
## Why Bob Adams (or Someone You Know) Is Healthy

### Stepping Along

**Step 1:** Use your main idea sentence and your idea map to help you write a one-paragraph composition. Use appropriate transitions to introduce each major point.

**Step 2:** Exchange compositions with a partner. With a pencil, lightly underline *twice* each major point in your partner's composition. Underline *once* each additional detail. Circle the transitions. As you read your partner's composition, think about these questions.

- Did your partner use details to support the major points?

- Did your partner use transitions appropriately?

- Can you give your partner any suggestions for improvement?

**Step 3:** Talk with your partner about your compositions. Try to agree on improvements that you can make.

**Step 4:** Rewrite your composition, making any changes you feel are necessary.

**Further steps:** As directed by your instructor.

# 9
## The Causes of Famine

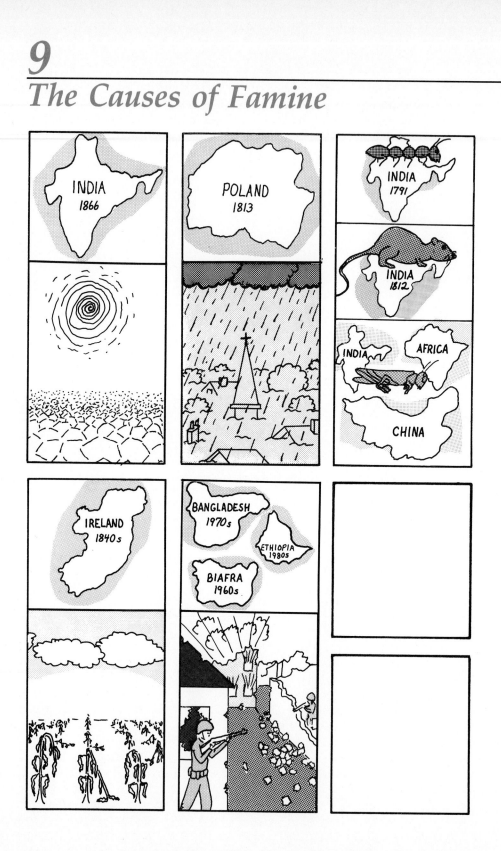

## PLANNING

A world relief organization wants to raise money to help the victims of famine. The organization plans to send a letter so people will understand why help is needed. The writer of the letter decides to give examples of serious famines from all over the world, both past and present. As he gathers ideas and information, he makes the following map. *Can you complete it using the pictures?*

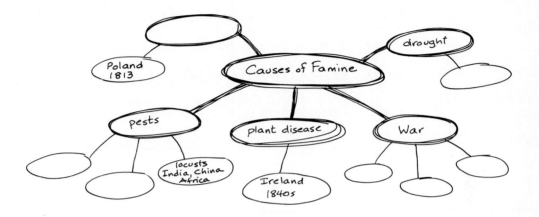

*How many major points does he have?* Notice how there is at least one additional detail for each major point.

## WRITING

Here is what he wrote. *Underline the main idea sentence. Circle the transitions that indicate a new major point.*

### ▌▐■ World Relief

   Famine, a serious problem today and in the past, has several different causes. One is drought. In 1967, a severe drought resulted in many deaths in India. Too much rainfall is another cause. In 1813, Poland suffered through a terrible famine because of weeks of continuous rain. Famine may also result from pests. Swarms of ants, for instance, attacked India's crops in 1791, and rats are responsible today for eating much of their stored grain. Locusts, another common pest, cause starvation all over the world, especially in Africa, India, and China. In addition, famine can occur when a plant disease destroys the main food supply. Almost 750,000 people starved to death in Ireland in the 1840s because of a potato disease. The major reason for widespread starvation, however, is war. In wartime, people are fighting instead of working in the fields. The enemy may bomb food storehouses and blow up roads so that food cannot be transported. The situations in Biafra in the 1960s, Bangladesh in the 1970s, and Ethiopia in the 1980s are modern examples of an old problem.

# ORGANIZATION

### Exercise 9A   Major Points and Additional Details

Read the following cause-effect paragraphs, and write at least one additional detail for each major point.

1.      People seldom stay in the old Brandmire Hotel anymore for several reasons.

First, the price of rooms is very high. *A double room costs over a hundred dollars, and a single costs over seventy-five dollars.* _____ Second, furnishings in

the rooms are frequently broken or in poor repair. _____

_____

_____

_____

_____

In addition, the hotel has no restaurant. _____

_____

_____

_____

Finally, the Brandmire Hotel is located in a dangerous section of town. _____

_____

_____

_____

_____

2.  There are many reasons English is a difficult language to learn. One reason is the use of prepositions. *For instance, in, on, and at are hard to learn. English speakers live "in" a city, "on" a street, and "at" an address!*

In addition, there are many odd idiomatic expressions. _____

_____

_____

_____

_____

A third reason for the difficulty of English is its irregular spelling. Many words in the language sound the same but are written differently. _____

_____

_____

_____

_____

## Main Idea Sentences

Remember that a main idea sentence for a cause-effect composition (1) tells the reader what the event or situation is and (2) mentions that there are causes or reasons for the situation.

### Exercise 9B

Read the following paragraphs carefully, and write a main idea sentence for each one.

1.  _____

    _____

    _____

    _____

    First, more infants survive today than in the past, so people don't need to have as many children now. Second, more women have jobs. They have fewer babies because it is difficult to care for children and work too. Perhaps one of the most important reasons Americans are having fewer children, however, is that the cost of raising a child is very high. Parents are afraid that they can't feed, clothe, and educate many children and are therefore limiting the size of their families.

2.  _____

    _____

    _____

    _____

    First, the population is increasing, and more gas and other fuels are being used. Second, the United States is not completely developing all its energy sources. For example, the use of coal has been limited because coal burning causes pollution. A third reason for the energy problem is America's dependence on oil from other countries. If these countries refuse to sell their oil, all Americans feel the effects. But probably the most important reason for the energy problem is that the United States has no acceptable alternate sources of energy. Both solar and nuclear power are possibilities, but solar power is not completely developed yet, and many people feel that nuclear power is dangerous.

**3.** 

_____

_____

_____

_____

One reason is that the husband's income is often no longer enough to cover expenses because the costs of housing, food, and education have increased. Another important reason is that there are more single-parent families. Due to increased divorce rates, more women live alone with their children and must work to support them. However, the most important reason of all is probably that the traditional role of women is changing. American women are no longer satisfied to stay at home in their kitchens. Instead, they are going outside their homes to pursue careers.

## GRAMMAR AND PUNCTUATION

### Showing Cause-Effect with *Because of*

You have learned that cause-effect is often expressed by two clauses connected with *because*. Cause can also be expressed by *because of + noun or noun phrase*. (A noun phrase is a phrase that functions as a noun.) Examine this pattern carefully, and compare it with *because + clause*. Notice the punctuation.

#### EXAMPLES

*Because + clause:*    Because there was a bad hailstorm, we couldn't get to work.
We couldn't get to work *because there was a bad hailstorm.*

*Because of +*
*noun/noun phrase:*    Because of a bad hailstorm, we couldn't get to work.
We couldn't get to work *because of a bad hailstorm.*

## Exercise 9C

Rewrite each sentence, replacing *because + clause* with *because of + noun phrase*. Punctuate correctly.

1.   *Because the divorce rate is high,* many children today are being raised by single parents.

*Because of the high divorce rate, many children today are being raised by single parents.*

2.   The school canceled the baseball game *because there was a thunderstorm warning.*

*The school canceled the baseball game because of a thunderstorm warning.*

3.   *Because its climate is bleak,* the Antarctic is uninhabited.

*Because of its bleak climate, the Antarctic is uninhabited*

4.   More than 22,000 lives were lost in Guatemala in 1976 *because there was a major earthquake.*

*Because of a major earthquake, More than 22,000 lives were lost in Guatemala in 1976.*

5.   They decided not to swim *because the current was rough.*

*Because of the rough current, they decided not to swim.*

6.   *Because the view is magnificent,* tourists enjoy visiting the Grand Canyon.

*Because of the magnificent view, tourists enjoy visiting the Grand Canyon.*

7.   Al Capone was often called "Scarface" *because there was a conspicuous scar on his cheek.*

8.   Many students apply to Yale University *because its reputation is excellent.*

## Exercise 9D

Fill in the blanks with an appropriate cause or effect. Use *because of* + *noun/noun phrase* when you fill in a cause.

1.  A famine occurred in Ireland in the 1840s _____

    _____ .

2.  _____ because

    of the bad weather.

3.  Saul wasn't accepted at the university _____

    _____ .

4.  _____ , Theresa

    always eats at Giordello's Restaurant.

5.  _____ because

    of the low prices.

6.  Paula wore a heavy sweater _____

    _____ .

7.  _____

    because of the bad traffic.

8.  Airports around the world are improving security systems _____

    _____ .

## Showing Cause-Effect with *So* and *Therefore*

The cause-effect relationship can also be expressed with *so* or *therefore*. Both introduce the effect clause. Notice the punctuation used with these words.

### EXAMPLE

Henrique received a large scholarship from his

government $\left\{ \begin{array}{l} \text{, so} \\ \text{; therefore,} \\ \text{. Therefore,} \end{array} \right\}$ he can attend a good university.

*So* and *therefore* have the same meaning, but *therefore* is used for more formal writing.

### Exercise 9E

Decide which sentence expresses the cause and which expresses the effect. Then combine the sentences using *so* or *therefore*. Practice all three ways. Change nouns to pronouns where necessary.

1.    Joy wants to be a top tennis player.
      Joy practices four hours a day.

      *Joy wants to be a top tennis player; therefore, she practices four hours a day.*

2.    Mr. Alvarez is allergic to smoke.
      He put a No Smoking sign in his office.

      *Because Mr. Alvarez is Allergic to smoke, he put a No smoking sign in his office.*

3.    The Wongs moved from Wisconsin to Florida.
      The Wongs dislike harsh winters.

      *Because the Wongs dislike harsh winters, The Wongs moved from wisconsin to Florida*

4.    Housing in the United States is becoming more expensive.
      There is an increase in homelessness.

5.    The world seems to be getting smaller.
      Transportation and communication are always improving.

Exercise 9F

As a review, finish the sentences by writing in your own ideas or feelings. Underline the appropriate word or phrase where you are given a choice of two.

1. _____ ; therefore,

   I am studying English.

2. I like/dislike the food in the United States because _____

   _____ .

3. _____ , so

   I'm in a good/bad mood today.

4. I study/do not study hard. Therefore, _____

   _____ .

5. _____ , so I

   got up early/late.

6. I feel tired/energetic today because _____

   _____ .

Exercise 9G   Review of Punctuation

Punctuate these sentences correctly. Some need no additional punctuation.

1. Because Ms. Divens was an excellent teacher her classes were always full.

2. Americans can vote when they are eighteen years old.

3. The bald eagle the symbol of the United States is very rare so the United States government protects it.

4. Ms. Nicholes has an ulcer therefore she never eats spicy foods.

5. Because of the high crime rate in many cities a large number of Americans prefer to live in the suburbs.

6. The University of Michigan has over 46000 students.

7. On March 10 1876 Alexander Graham Bell first demonstrated the telephone.

8. The vaccine for rabies was discovered in 1885 by Louis Pasteur a French scientist.

# Student Plan and Composition 9

Develop your topic, or choose one of the following for your final cause-effect composition. Consider your fellow students as your audience.

1. Causes of air pollution

2. Why I like (or dislike) living in this city

3. Why I like (or dislike) attending this college

4. *MORE CHALLENGING:* People who live in large cities have a shorter life expectancy than people who live in small towns. Why do you think this is so?

## Stepping Along

**Step 1:** After choosing your topic, divide into pairs or small groups according to the topic you have chosen. Discuss the topic together. Try to generate as many ideas as possible.

**Step 2:** Together, write a plan or make a map of your ideas. Remember to add additional details to each of your major points.

**Step 3:** On your own, write a composition using your plan or map and main idea sentence. Remember to use transitions of addition (*first, also, in addition,* and so on) to introduce your major points.

**Step 4:** Exchange compositions with a new partner. As you read your partner's composition, think about these questions.

- What do you like best about the composition?

- Is everything in the composition clear to you?

- Has your partner supported each major point with at least one additional detail?

- Are transitions used appropriately?

- Can you give your partner any suggestions for improvement?

**Step 5:** Talk with your partner about your compositions. Try to agree on improvements that you can make.

**Step 6:** Rewrite your composition, making any changes that you feel are necessary.

**Further steps:** As directed by your instructor.

# Unit 4

# Comparing and Contrasting

Comparing and contrasting is something all of us frequently do. When you decide, for instance, whether to buy your friend's used motorcycle or a new one, whether to attend the university in New York or the one in California, or whether to rent the apartment near the university or the one downtown, you compare and contrast. **Comparing** means thinking or writing about the *similarities* between two things or people; **contrasting** means thinking or writing about their *differences*.

When you compare and contrast, you can organize your material in several different ways. In this unit, you will learn two simple arrangements.

Suppose you are interested in showing the differences between airplanes and helicopters. You will then write a contrast composition. When you are contrasting, however, it is effective to mention also the similarities between the two things you are contrasting. You should mention these similarities in your main idea sentence. If you wish, you may develop these similarities in a separate paragraph before going on to the differences.

One way to arrange your material (after writing your main idea sentence and discussing the similarities) is to write about airplanes in one paragraph and to write about helicopters in the next. If you mention a particular point in the airplane paragraph, you must mention the same point in the helicopter paragraph, and *in the same order*. Study the following outline, which shows this kind of organization.

Introduction

(I. Similarities between airplanes and helicopters)

II. Airplanes
    A. Shape and design
    B. Speed
    C. Direction of takeoff and flight

III. Helicopters
    A. Shape and design
    B. Speed
    C. Direction of takeoff and flight

Conclusion

A second way to organize this material is to discuss a particular point about airplanes and then immediately discuss the same point about helicopters. This is called a point-by-point arrangement. An outline of this arrangement follows.

Introduction

(I. Similarities between airplanes and helicopters)

II. Differences between airplanes and helicopters
    A. Shape and design
        1. Airplanes
        2. Helicopters
    B. Speed
        1. Airplanes
        2. Helicopters
    C. Direction of takeoff and flight
        1. Airplanes
        2. Helicopters

Conclusion

When you become a more experienced writer, you may want to develop each point into a separate paragraph, but in this unit, you will use a single paragraph for your point-by-point arrangements.

When you want to emphasize the *similarities* between two things or two people, you may use these same arrangements.

Both students and professionals frequently need to compare and contrast in order to explain something. A physics student, for instance, might explain fission and fusion by pointing out their differences and similarities. Similarly, an economist might find it useful to explain this year's table of economic growth by comparing and contrasting it with last year's table.

## 10

Adjetive —

# My Two Brothers

## PLANNING

In Peter Bustamente's psychology class, the professor raised this question: Is heredity or environment more important in personality development? Peter feels that neither of them plays a great role. To prove his point to the teacher, he decided to write about his two brothers, Nick and Joe. First he listed these differences.

| (NICK) | (JOE) |
|---|---|
| – has long, curly hair + beard. | – short, straight hair / no beard |
| – wears jeans + T-shirt | – suit + tie |
| – is a cook | – businessman |
| – likes to go by bicycle | – always drives car |
| – likes movies + football | – dancing + soccer |
| – lives in studio apt. (alone) | – large, suburban house (with family + pet) |

*phisical charact.*

*job*

*hobbies interests*

Notice that Peter arranged his major points in the same order. First he mentioned the *appearance* of Nick and Joe, then their *clothes*, then their *professions*, and so on.

## WRITING

This is his final draft. Notice that his composition has both an introduction (first paragraph) and a *conclusion* (last paragraph). You will learn more about introductions in this lesson and about conclusions in lesson 12. *What information does Peter put in the second paragraph? in the third paragraph?*

---

### My Two Brothers

Most people assume that sisters and brothers have many things in common. This is not always true. Both my brothers, Nick and Joe, have the same parents and the same background, but they differ considerably in appearance and lifestyle.

Nick, the younger one, has long, curly hair and a beard. He usually dresses casually in blue jeans and a T-shirt. He is a cook in a small restaurant. Because the restaurant is near his home, he rides his bicycle to work. In his free time, Nick goes to movies and plays football. He lives alone in the city in a studio apartment.

My brother Joe, on the other hand, looks more conservative than Nick. He has shorter, straighter hair. He has a mustache but no beard. His clothes are also more conservative than Nick's are. Because he is a businessman, he wears a suit and tie to work. He drives his car to his downtown office every day. In his spare time, he goes dancing and plays soccer. Joe lives in a large house in the suburbs with his wife, their children, and a cat.

My friends cannot believe that Nick and Joe are brothers because they seem so different.

# ORGANIZATION

*study*

## Main Idea Sentences

A main idea sentence for a composition that compares and contrasts should tell the reader (1) what two things or people are being compared and contrasted and (2) whether the composition will emphasize the similarities or the differences between them. Even if you wish to stress the differences in your main idea sentence, you should still mention the similarities, and vice versa. Often, words like *but* and *however* are used to connect the two parts of a main idea sentence for a compare/contrast composition.

### EXAMPLES

Study carefully these examples of main idea sentences for compare/contrast compositions. Answer the following questions for each.

- What two things or people are being *compared* or *contrasted?*

- Will the composition emphasize the *similarities* or the *differences* between them?

*Disneyland and Disneyworld are both products of the imagination of the same man, Walt Disney,* **but** *the two parks offer very different types of entertainment.*

*The political systems of the United States and my country seem different at first,* **but** *they actually have some <u>striking</u> similarities.*

<u>strong</u>

*Many people think that humans have little in common with sea animals;* **however,** *scientists have shown that the dolphin resembles us in many ways.*

## Exercise 10A

Read each short composition carefully. Then circle the best main idea sentence for each.

1.   **a.** Airplanes and helicopters are both important forms of air travel, but there are great differences between them.

   **b.** Airplanes and helicopters are both important forms of air transportation; however, they do not travel at the same speeds.

   **c.** Airplanes and helicopters have very different shapes, but both carry passengers.

Airplanes have long, slender bodies with wings. They travel extremely fast, reaching speeds of over 1,875 miles (3,000 kilometers) per hour. Airplanes take off horizontally and can move in a forward direction only. They need a lot of space for takeoff and landing. Airplanes regularly carry several hundred passengers.

Helicopters, on the other hand, have round bodies and propellers rather than wings. They move at much slower speeds than airplanes. They take off vertically and can move in any direction. Helicopters require a very small takeoff or landing space. Most helicopters carry only two to five passengers.

Dferences

2.   **a.** The cities in the United States are different from those in other countries.

   **b.** Los Angeles and New York are both large American cities, but they differ in major ways.

   **c..** New York and Los Angeles are both important cities in the United States; however, they are located on opposite coasts and have different-sized buildings.

New York City is located on the East Coast of the United States. It is filled with skyscrapers that are concentrated in a relatively small area of 319 square miles (829 square kilometers). New York is known as the fashion center of the United States and also contains most of the publishing houses that select and print the nation's books.

Los Angeles is on the West Coast of the United States. This city is spread out over a much larger area of 464 square miles (1,206 square kilometers), and its buildings are much lower than the buildings in New York. Los Angeles is an important industrial center for the manufacture of aircraft and airplane parts. Los Angeles is also the capital of the movie industry.

3.   **a.** Hitler was a dictator of Germany, but Mussolini was a dictator of Italy.

   **b.** Hitler and Mussolini ruled different countries; however, they both wanted power.

   **c.** Hitler and Mussolini were heads of two different countries, but their dictatorships had much in common.

Hitler, a dictator who believed in the superiority of the German people, built up Germany's military strength during the 1930s. His aim was to dominate Europe. He arrested people by the millions and sent them to concentration camps or executed them. Hitler involved Europe in a catastrophic war. He is believed to have committed suicide when it became clear that Germany had lost.

Similarly, the dictator Mussolini craved power and wanted all the men of Italy to be soldiers. His aim was to build Italy into a great empire. Like Hitler, Mussolini kept control by means of murder, exile, and prison camps. He joined Hitler in the war and, when Italy was losing, was shot by his Italian opponents.

## Introductions

Now that your compositions will be more than one paragraph in length, they should have an introduction. In short compositions, such as those you will be writing for this course, the introduction is usually a few sentences in length and generally includes the main idea sentence. A good introduction makes the reader want to continue reading.

An introduction introduces the subject generally. Then it specifies, in a main idea sentence, what particular points will be discussed in the composition. The introduction in the composition on page 107 introduces the subject of sisters and brothers in general and then goes on to talk about two particular brothers, Nick and Joe.

There are different ways to write an introduction. One way is to begin with a common belief and show that it is not always true. The main idea sentence then gives the particular points that will be discussed in the composition to prove that the common belief is not always true. This method is the one that has been used for the composition.

> *Most people assume that sisters and brothers have many things in common. This is not always true. Both my brothers, Nick and Joe, have the same parents and the same background, but they differ considerably in appearance and lifestyle.*

Another way of writing an introduction is to begin with a very general idea and to narrow it down in the main idea sentence. The above introduction could also have been written in this way.

> *Some brothers are as different as night and day. Both my brothers, Nick and Joe, have the same parents and the same background, but they differ considerably in appearance and lifestyle.*

Exercise 10B

Write a short introduction for each of the three compositions in Exercise 10A. Begin your introduction with a common belief or a general statement, as explained above. Then continue with the main idea sentence. You may have to make some small changes in your main idea sentence.

1. _____

_____

_____

_____

_____

_____

_____

2. _____

_____

_____

_____

_____

_____

_____

3. _____

_____

_____

_____

_____

_____

_____

## Finding Similarities and Differences

It is important to examine carefully the two things you want to compare or contrast. The following exercise will give you practice in looking for similarities and differences.

### Exercise 10C

Look at the pictures below. The people or things pictured have similarities as well as differences. List at least three similarities and three differences for each pair of pictures.

**Julie**                    **Sandy**

1.      *Similarities*

~~Both of the girls. (them) (x and y )~~

a. _They wear glasses_

b. _They are the same age_

c. _They have long hair_

*Differences*

a. Julie: _wears oval glasses but_

Sandy: _wears_

b. Julie: _is thin but San_

Sandy: _is havy_

c. Julie: _has a oval face but_

Sandy: _has a roud face_

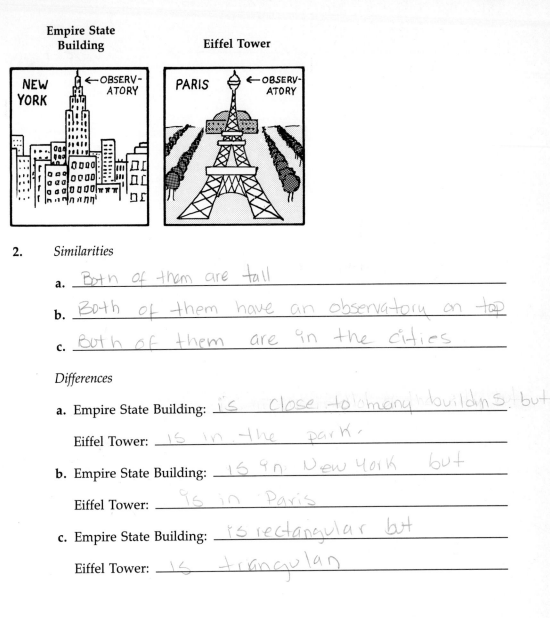

**2.** *Similarities*

a. Both of them are tall

b. Both of them have an observatory on top

c. Both of them are in the cities

*Differences*

a. Empire State Building: is close to many buildins but

Eiffel Tower: is in the park.

b. Empire State Building: is in New York but

Eiffel Tower: is in Paris

c. Empire State Building: is rectangular but

Eiffel Tower: is triangular

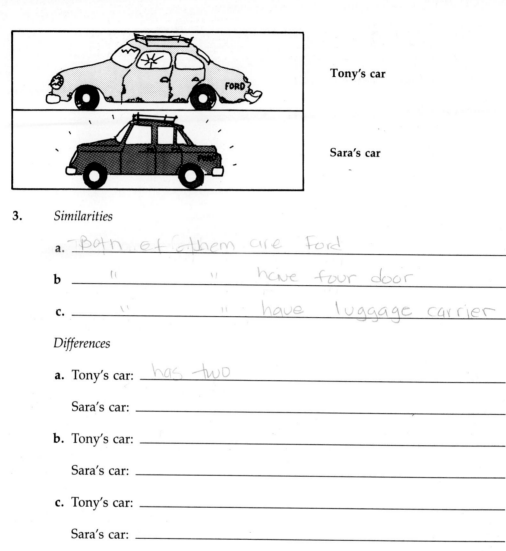

Tony's car

Sara's car

**3.**     *Similarities*

a. Both of them are Ford

b    "          "    have four door

c. _____"_____"__ have luggage carrier

*Differences*

a. Tony's car: has two

   Sara's car: _____

b. Tony's car: _____

   Sara's car: _____

c. Tony's car: _____

   Sara's car: _____

**Book 1**          **Book 2**

6.95
COLLEGE
CHEMISTRY
BY
J.R. HILL

SLATER, INC

12.95
HIGH SCHOOL
BIOLOGY
BY
J.R. HILL

SLATER, INC.

**4.**     *Similarities*

a.    ~~both of them~~ They are written by J.R. Hill ~~writter~~

b.    They are the same big.

c.    The edptorial is slater Inc, for both.
      Both of them are publishe by Stater Inc.
      are science.

*Differences*

**a.** Book 1: ___The price is 6.95___

Book 2: ___the price is 12.95___

**b.** Book 1: ___The grade is college___

Book 2: ___The grade is high school___

**c.** Book 1: ___The area is chemestry___

Book 2: ___The area Is Biology___

## Using *Both* for Similarities

When two things or people have something in common, we often use *both* to compare them. *Both* is grammatically plural, so it requires the plural verb form.

### EXAMPLES

Julie has long hair. Sandy has long hair.

*Both* Julie and Sandy (*Both* of them) have long hair.

Julie and Sandy *both* (They *both*) have long hair.

When using a form of the verb *to be* in this type of sentence, *both* appears after the verb.

Julie and Sandy are *both* students.

## Exercise 10D

Write sentences using *both* for some of the similarities you found in the pictures in Exercise 10C.

1. *Both Julie and Sandy wear glasses.*
   *Julie and Sandy both wear glasses.*

2.

3.

4.

5.

6.

## Using *But* for Differences

When we want to show that two things are different or contrasting, we often use *but* to show the contrast. Notice the punctuation used with *but*.

### EXAMPLES

Nick's hair is long, *but* Joe's is short.

Nick lives alone, *but* Joe lives with his family.

## Exercise 10E

Write sentences using *but* for some of the differences you found in the pictures in Exercise 10C.

1. *The Empire State Building is made of stone, but the Eiffel Tower is made of steel.*

2.

3.

4.

5.

6.

## Transitions Showing Contrast: *On the Other Hand*

Composition 10 has two major parts: the paragraph about Nick and the paragraph about Joe. A transition (*on the other hand*) is used to connect these two contrasting paragraphs. Underline this transition in the composition.

*On the other hand* can also be used to connect sentences that show the contrast between two things or people.

### EXAMPLES

Gold is a precious and rare metal. *On the other hand,* iron is cheap and abundant.

Lily always dresses up. Her sister, *on the other hand,* usually wears blue jeans.

### Exercise 10F

Use *on the other hand* to show the contrasting relationship in the following pairs of sentences.

1.    Susan loves cats. Her husband hates them.

*Susan loves cats. Her husband, on the other hand, hates them.*

2.    The winters in New York City are cold and snowy. The summers are hot and humid.

3.    Salomon speaks English very well. His wife speaks it poorly.

4.    The University of Pennsylvania is located in an urban area. Pennsylvania State University is in a rural area.

5.    Most of the earth's surface is covered by water. The surface of the moon is entirely dry.

6.    In the United States, a nod means yes. In Bulgaria, it means no.

## GRAMMAR AND PUNCTUATION

### Comparatives

When we contrast two things that are different, we often use the **comparative degree** of adjectives.

For one-syllable adjectives (*tall, thin, big*), add *-er* to the adjective, and use *than* after the adjective. Double the final consonant if the adjective ends in a single consonant preceded by a single vowel (*big — bigger, fat — fatter*).

John is tall*er than* Nat (is).
John is bigg*er than* Nat (is).

For two-syllable adjectives ending in *y* (*hap-py, la-zy*), add *-er* to the adjective, and use *than* after it. Change *y* to *i* if a consonant precedes it.

Mr. Rossi is happi*er than* Ms. Roter (is).
She is angri*er than* he (is).

For most other two-syllable and all three-syllable adjectives, place *more* in front of the adjective and *than* after it.

She seems *more* intelligent *than* he (does).
That watch is *more* expensive *than* this one (is).

## Exercise 10G

Give the number of syllables in each of the following words. Then write the comparative form of each.

1. expensive   _3_ _more expensive_

2. easy   ____ _____

3. fast   ____ _____

4. crowded   ____ _____

5. friendly   ____ _____

6. thin   ____ _____

7. dirty   ____ _____

8. successful   ____ _____

9. happy   ____ _____

10. handsome   ____ _____

11. honest   ____ _____

12. hot   ____ _____

13. difficult   ____ _____

14. curly   ____ _____

15. clean   ____ _____

**Exercise 10H**

Write one comparative sentence for each of the words or phrases in parentheses.
Use a form of the verb *to be* in all your sentences.

1.  Alaska has an area of 589,757 square miles (1,527,469 square kilometers). Texas
    has an area of 267,338 square miles (692,405 square kilometers). (*big, small*)

    *Alaska is bigger than Texas.*
    *Texas is smaller than Alaska.*

2.  The Sears Tower in Chicago is 1,454 feet (436 meters) tall. The World Trade
    Center in New York City is 1,353 feet (406 meters) tall. (*tall, short*)

    The Sears Tower in Chicago is taller than the
    World Trade Center in New York City.
    The World Trade Center in New York City is shorter
    that the Sears Tower in Chicago.

3.  Joan and Bill are both students at the university. Joan studies five hours a
    night. Bill studies only a few hours each weekend. (*lazy, industrious*)

    Joan is more industrius than Bill.
    Bill is more Lazy than Joan.

4.  Quibdo, Colombia, has an average rainfall of 345 inches (863 centimeters) a
    year. Bataques, Mexico, has an average annual rainfall of 1.2 inches (3 cen-
    timeters) per year. (*dry, wet*)

    Quibdo Colombia is wetter than Bataques, Mexico.
    Bataques, Mexico is drier than Quibdo Colombia.

5.  Bob weighs 120 pounds (54 kilograms), but his friend Rafael weighs
    200 pounds (90 kilograms). (*light, heavy*)

    Bob is lighter than Rafael.
    Rafael is heavier than Bob.

6.  A Volkswagen Rabbit can run 40 miles (64 kilometers) on a gallon of gas. A
    Cadillac, however, gets only 15 miles (24 kilometers) per gallon. (*cheap to oper-
    ate, expensive to operate*)

7.  Maria is thirty years old. Mohammed is twenty-eight. (*old, young*)

    Maria is older than Mohammed.
    Mohammed is younger than Maria.

# Student Plan 10
## *Two Sisters*

Imagine you have met two very different women at a party. You are surprised later when you find out they are sisters. You discuss these differences in a letter to a friend. Use these pictures of Joyce and Karen in preparing to write about their differences. Make a plan on the opposite page. Work with a partner if you wish.

**Helpful vocabulary:**

| Joyce | Karen |
|---|---|
| sweater | wear (suit, glasses) |
| jeans | lawyer |
| mechanic | go to the theater |
| ride a bicycle | pets |

*Main idea sentence\** _____

_____

_____

_____

_____

\*You may want to write your main idea sentence after you finish the plan.

*Make a Plan Here*

# Student Composition 10
## Two Sisters

### Stepping Along

**Step 1:** Use your plan to help you write a composition. In addition to your major paragraphs, write an introduction using your main idea sentence.

**Step 2:** Exchange compositions with a partner. As you read your partner's composition, think about these questions.

- Is everything in your partner's composition clear to you?

- Is paragraphing correct?

- Is a transition used to introduce the second major paragraph?

- Is the comparative form used? If so, has your partner used it correctly? Underline lightly any uses of the comparative, and decide if the form is correct.

- Can you give your partner at least three suggestions for improvement?

**Step 3:** Talk with your partner about your compositions. Try to agree on improvements you can make.

**Step 4:** Rewrite your composition, making any changes you feel are necessary.

**Further steps:** As directed by your instructor.

# 11
## Two Houses for Sale

**The House on Duncan Street**

**The House on Arla Street**

## PLANNING

The Bitar family is moving from New York to Pittsburgh. A friend, Carl Lee, is looking for a house for them in Pittsburgh. He is going to write a letter to the Bitars to tell them about two houses he has seen. First, he looked at his notes. (*There is some important information missing. Can you add it?*)

House on Duncan

- brick
- 2 bedrooms, bath, living room, kitchen, dining room
- car port
- big backyard
- March heating - $40

House on Arla

- wood (needs paint!)
- 2 bedrooms, bath, living room, kitchen, dining room
- car port
- no backyard
- March heating - $120

Then to organize his notes, Carl arranged things according to *similarities* and *differences*.

Similarities
- Both have same 6 rooms
- Both have carports
- "      cost $90,000.

Differences

| Duncan | Arla |
|---|---|
| - brick | - wood (needs paint!) |
| - big yard | - no yard |
| - low heating bills | - high heating bills |

# WRITING

Here is Carl's letter to the Bitars. *After he compares and contrasts the two houses, what conclusion does he reach?*

April 1

Dear Lisa and Alec,

I've looked at the two houses that Century Realty has for sale. I like both of them. When I first saw them, they seemed similar; however, there are some important differences you should be aware of.

One obvious similarity is their interiors. Both the house on Duncan and the one on Arla have two bedrooms, a large kitchen, a living room, a dining room, and a full bathroom. Neither house has a garage, but each has a carport on one side. Also, both houses are selling for the same price—$90,000.

I noticed considerable differences in the homes, however. The house on Duncan is brick, so it won't need much upkeep. The one on Arla, on the other hand, is wood, and it needs to be painted. The house on Duncan has a big backyard with a lot of trees. It's ideal for your children. The house on Arla has no backyard at all. The most important difference is probably their heating costs. The monthly heating bills of the residence on Arla are much higher.

I won't make a decision until you see these homes, but I'm sure you're going to agree with me. The two houses share several similarities. However, because of the differences, I believe the one on Duncan is a better value.

I look forward to hearing from you soon.

Sincerely,

*Carl*

Carl

# ORGANIZATION

### Exercise 11A   Irrelevant Sentences

Read the following paragraphs. Find the sentence in each that does not support the main idea sentence. Cross it out.

1.  Mosquitoes and houseflies differ in appearance and habits, but the two insects share many similarities. First, both are typical of hot, humid climates. Both insects suck their food. Houseflies suck their food from various sources, while most mosquitoes suck blood from animals and people. Both insects can cling to smooth surfaces and even walk upside down across ceilings. Finally, both can spread serious diseases. Houseflies spread typhoid, tuberculosis, and cholera, and mosquitoes carry malaria and yellow fever. Mosquitoes that carry malaria bite at night.

2.  La Cuisine serves French food, and Minutello's serves Italian food; however, the two restaurants have many things in common. Both their dining rooms are clean and elegant. Also, their meals are carefully prepared and reasonably priced. Italian food is as delicious as French food. In addition, the service is excellent at both restaurants. Their waiters are friendly and polite. Finally, both La Cuisine and Minutello's are open until very late at night.

3.  Moths and butterflies are closely related and look very much alike; however, they differ from each other in four ways. First, most moths are active at night, but most butterflies are active during the day. Butterflies fly from flower to flower sucking their "nectar." Second, when moths rest, they spread their wings out. Butterflies, in contrast, hold their wings straight up. Their antennae are also different. The antennae of most moths are hairlike and pointed. All butterflies have knobs at the end of their antennae. Finally, the bodies of most moths are thick. The bodies of butterflies are thin.

# GRAMMAR AND PUNCTUATION

### Transitions·Showing Contrast: *However*

*However* expresses contrast. It can connect two paragraphs or two sentences. Notice the punctuation used with the different positions of *however*. *However* is used mostly in formal writing.

#### EXAMPLE

Alaska is a large state. *However*, it has a small population.

Alaska is a large state; *however*, it has a small population.

Alaska is a large state. It has a small population, *however*.

### Exercise 11B

Underline all uses of *however* in Composition 11. Decide which ones connect sentences and which ones connect paragraphs.

### Exercise 11C

Connect the following sentences using *however*. Try to use *however* in each position at least once, and use correct punctuation.

1.  The food in the Broadway Cafe is excellent. The service is poor.

    *The food in the Broadway Cafe is excellent; however, the service is poor.*

2.  Athens is a very old city. It has many modern buildings.

    Athens is a very old city; however, it has many modern buildings.

3.  It is warm outside. Our house is cold.

    It is warm outside. However, Our house is cold.

4.     Chuck doesn't study much. He does well in school.

*Chuck doesn't study much; however, He does well in school.*

5.     The coast of Maine is crowded in the summer. Very few people go there in
       the winter.

*The coast of Maine is crowded in the summer. However, Very few people go there in the winter.*

6.     The bite of a coral snake is nearly painless. It can cause death.

*The bite of a coral snake is nearly painles. However, It can cause death.*

## Exercise 11D  Review of *But* and *However*

Decide which of the following pairs of sentences express contrast. Combine such
sentences with *but* or *however*. Write *no* after the sentences that do not express contrast.

1.     Ostriches have wings. They cannot fly.

*Ostriches have wings but they cannot fly*

2.     We are going to buy a used car. We cannot afford a new one.  *no*

3.     Thomas Edison was not a successful student. He became one of the most
       important inventors in history.

*Thomas Edison was not a successful student; however, he became one of the most important inventors in historia.*

4.     Smoking cigarettes is unhealthy. Many people smoke.

*Smoking cigarettes is unhealthy, but many people smoke.*

5.     They were driving fast. They got a speeding ticket.    no

6.     The spider looks very delicate. It can survive almost anywhere.

7.     He went out to eat. Then he went to a movie.    no

8.     The price is high. We are still going to buy the house.

   The price is high, but we are still going
   to buy the house.

9.     The steamship *Titanic* sank. It struck an iceberg.

10.    She doesn't like pizza. She ate some last night.

   She doesn't like pizza, but she
   ate some last night.

## Using *Neither* for Similarities

You have learned that when two things or people have something in common, we can use *both* to compare them. When two people or things have something negative in common, we often use *neither*. In the following examples, *neither* is the subject of the sentence. It is grammatically singular and takes a singular verb form.

### EXAMPLES

The house on Arla does not have a garage.

The house on Duncan does not have a garage.

*Neither* of the houses has a garage.

*Neither* house has a garage.

Note that *of the* can be dropped. The plural noun then becomes singular.

## Exercise 11E

Combine the information in the following pairs of sentences by using *neither*. Write each sentence two ways.

1.  Mr. Schaeffer doesn't have a car.
    Mr. Jonescu doesn't have a car.

    *Neither of the men has a car.*

    *Neither man has a car.*

2.  My sister Anne doesn't like disco music.
    My sister Karen doesn't like disco music.

    _____

    _____

3.    The state of Hawaii is not part of the mainland of the United States.
      The state of Alaska is not part of the mainland of the United States.

      _____

      _____

4.    The house on the corner is not for sale.
      The house across the street is not for sale.

      _____

      _____

5.    The shoe store is not open on Sundays.
      The hardware store is not open on Sundays.

      _____

      _____

6.    The planet Mercury does not have any satellites.
      The planet Venus does not have any satellites.

      _____

      _____

7.    The history teacher doesn't live near the university.
      The biology teacher doesn't live near the university.

      _____

      _____

Exercise 11F    Review of *Both* and *Neither*

Use the picture to write sentences with *both* and *neither*.

*Both*

1. Both Jack and Fred have bats.

2.

3.

4.

*Neither*

1.

2.

3.

# Student Plan 11
## Two Items for Sale and
## Two Apartments for Rent

A. Are you considering buying something big (perhaps a TV, a bike, a car, or a computer)? Make a plan to compare and contrast two models of the item you are looking at.

OR

B. Imagine that a friend from another city is moving to your area. The friend has asked you to look at two rental apartments that were advertised in the newspaper. You will be comparing the two to show your friend which one is a better value.

Discuss the pictures with a partner or a small group. Use the pictures and your own ideas to complete the plan on the opposite page. You should have at least three major points for each paragraph.

**The Apartment on Hill Avenue**

*alicia yenet*

## The Apartment on Wood Street

TWO-BEDROOM APARTMENT $520.00 UTILITIES INCLUDED

WOOD ST.

### Helpful vocabulary:

| | |
|---|---|
| rent | dishwasher |
| second floor | basement |
| building | laundry facilities |
| parking lot | do the laundry |
| wall-to-wall carpeting | Laundromat |

*Main idea sentence* _____

_____

_____

*You may want to write your main idea sentence after you finish the plan.

*Similarities*

*Differences*

# Student Composition 11
## Two Items for Sale and Two Apartments for Rent

### Stepping Along

**Step 1:** Use your plan to help you write a composition. In addition to your major paragraphs, write an introduction paragraph using your main idea sentence. Use *neither* at least once, and write appropriate transitions.

**Step 2:** Exchange compositions with a partner. As you read your partner's composition, think about these questions.

- Did your partner follow all the directions in step 1?

- Is everything in your partner's composition clear to you?

- Can you give your partner at least three suggestions for improvement?

**Step 3:** Talk with your partner about your compositions. Try to agree on improvements you can make.

**Step 4:** Rewrite your composition, making any changes you feel are necessary.

**Further steps:**  As directed by your instructor.

## PLANNING

A French woman, Sophie Gabriel, is a student in Washington, D.C. Her university newspaper has asked her to write about her hometown, Paris, as compared to Washington. Before writing, she organized her ideas according to the *differences* and the *similarities* between the cities.

```
PARIS                  WASHINGTON
(Differences)
- 2,000 + years old    - about 200 years old
- 2,000,000 people     - 638,000 people

(Similarities)
- They are political centers
- They have symmetrical layouts
- They both have many museums, parks, etc.
- Both are tourist centers
```

## WRITING

Sophie's final draft appeared in the newspaper like this. How is it different from her plan?

---

# Two Cities

Sophie Gabriel

It is difficult to imagine that a large, old city and a new, small one could be similar at all. However, anyone who has seen Paris and Washington knows that this is possible. The two cities differ in age and population, but they share many similarities.

Of course, Paris is the older city. It is over 2,000 years old. Washington, in contrast, is very young. It is about 200 years old. The population of Paris (2,000,000) is also much larger than Washington's population (638,000).

Although these important differences exist, the cities are strikingly similar. First, both cities are the political centers of their countries. The president of France lives in the heart of Paris, in the Elysee Palace. Likewise, the president of the United States lives in the heart of Washington, in the White House. The French National Assembly meets in Paris, in the Palais Bourbon. The Congress of the United States has its meeting place in Washington, in the Capitol Building. Second, the two cities look similar. L'Enfant, the French engineer who designed Washington, was greatly influenced by the layout of Paris. For this reason, many of the buildings and monuments in Washington are symmetrically located in view of one another, just as they are in Paris. Both cities are also the sites of magnificent monuments; important historical landmarks; fine museums; beautiful parks; and broad, tree-lined avenues. Finally, tourism is as important for Washington as it is for Paris. Every year, millions of tourists from all over the world flock to these cities.

In conclusion, Paris and Washington share numerous similarities. Besides being political and tourist centers, the cities have a similar look.

# ORGANIZATION

## Transitions Showing Contrast and Similarity

You already know some of the transitions used to connect two contrasting sentences or paragraphs. *In contrast* is another transition you can use to show contrast. Note the punctuation used.

### EXAMPLES

Paris is over 2,000 years old. Washington, *in contrast,* is very young.

Paris is over 2,000 years old. *In contrast,* Washington is very young.

There are also transitions that introduce similarities between two sentences or two paragraphs. Two of them are *likewise* (used in the composition on page 141) and *similarly.* A comma is usually used after these transitions.

### EXAMPLES

The president of France lives in the capital of France.

*Likewise,*
*Similarly,* the president of the United States lives in the capital of the United States.

## Exercise 12A

The following is *not* a good composition because none of the sentences that introduce similarity or contrast contain transitions. Read the composition, and decide which sentences could be improved by using transitions. Then rewrite the composition using *in contrast, on the other hand, however, likewise,* or *similarly* where appropriate.

---

Hotels and motels are the most common kinds of accommodations for travelers in the United States. Although both provide housing and a variety of services, they do differ in some respects.

Hotels and motels serve their guests in similar ways. Hotels, for instance, have restaurants and cafeterias. Many motels provide facilities for meals. In addition, hotels often have swimming pools, golf courses, or tennis courts. Many motels offer various recreational facilities.

In spite of these similarities, hotels and motels are different. First, hotels are generally larger than motels; some have over thirty floors. Motels have only one or two floors. In addition, most hotels have ballrooms for conventions and weddings. Motels usually don't. Most hotels are located in downtown sections. Motels are found along highways, frequently at intersections or at exits to highways. Perhaps the main difference between hotels and motels is the way you can get to your room. In a hotel, you have to go through a lobby to reach your room. In a motel, you can drive your car up to the door of your room.

Hotels and motels, then, provide a variety of similar services, but their size, location, and room arrangement are often different.

---

*Rewritten Composition*

_____

_____

_____

_____

_____

_____

_____

_____

_____

_____

_____

_____

_____

_____

_____

_____

_____

_____

_____

_____

_____

_____

_____

_____

_____

## Main Idea Sentences and Introductions

The following phrases will be useful to you when you are writing main idea sentences for compare/contrast compositions.

X and Y *have many things in common.*  They have a lot of
X and Y *have few things in common.*

X and Y *are very similar.*
X and Y *are very different.*

X and Y *share many similarities.*
X and Y *have many differences.*

X *resembles* Y.
X and Y *differ.*

X *is similar to* Y.
X *is different from* Y.

Remember that when you compare and contrast, your main idea sentence will contain two parts. Even if it has the two parts, however, it may not be suitable, as the following example shows.

> *Poor:    The sculptors Michelangelo and Rodin are different; however, they have many things in common.*    It doesn't make sense

This main idea sentence tells (1) what is being compared and (2) what will be emphasized. It does not give the reader any information, however, about *what* is similar or *what* is different between the two artists. Just saying that two things or people are different but similar, or similar but different, is not enough. The following example *is* an acceptable main idea sentence because it gives some introductory information on *what* is different between the sculptor (they lived in different centuries and different countries) and *what* is similar (their works of art).

> *Better:    The sculptors Michelangelo and Rodin lived in different centuries and different countries; however, their works of art have many things in common.*

sin embargo
In the above example, both parts of the main idea sentence are expanded, but it is often sufficient to expand only one part.

If you were writing a longer composition, you would expand this main idea sentence into an introduction. You could begin with a common belief and then show it is not true.

> *Most people do not see many similarities between Michelangelo and Rodin. It is true that the sculptors lived in different centuries and different countries; however, their works of art have many things in common.*

Or you might begin with a general statement.

> *Michelangelo and Rodin are two of history's greatest sculptors. They lived in different centuries and different countries; however, their works of art have many things in common.*

Focus —
is what are you giving
the importance —

### Exercise 12B

Read each composition carefully, and write an introduction for it. Remember that an introduction must include a main idea sentence.

1. _Lions are wild and cats are domesticated however, they share many similarities._

 

 

Lions are large, fierce, powerful beasts that look very frightening. They are known as "kings of the jungle." Cats, on the other hand, are small, quiet, gentle animals that do not look threatening. They are completely domesticated.

However, both animals are members of the same family, the Felidae family. Both are covered with the same soft fur and have the same long whiskers on their face. Both the lion and the cat are meat-eating mammals. They are also well-coordinated; they can climb easily and usually land on their feet after a fall. They move quickly and quietly on soft, padded feet. Finally, both animals are very clean because they wash themselves frequently with their tongues.

2. _Most people don't know that American + European table manners are different. French and Americans agree that good table manners are important even in their daily lives; however they disagree about something_

When eating, both the French and Americans enjoy table conversation. Both eat with knives and forks. Neither considers it polite to talk with food in the mouth.

There are many differences in table manners, however. The French keep the fork in the left hand while eating meat; many Americans don't. In France, both hands should be kept on the table while eating. In the United States, the left hand may be on the lap. The French break off a piece of bread with their fingers and eat it. Americans, in contrast, pick up the whole piece. Finally, the French eat fruit with a knife and fork. Americans usually use their fingers.

3.  

 

 

 

Camels are large and have one or two humps on their backs. Llamas, in contrast, are small and have no humps. Camels live in the deserts of North Africa, Arabia, and Mongolia. Llamas live in South America.

The two animals, however, have much in common. First, they belong to the same class of animals. They are hoofed, four-legged ruminants. Second, both can be bad-tempered. Camels bite and kick when they get angry, and llamas spit at their enemy. Finally, both are commonly used in dry regions for transporting people or burdens because they can live for weeks without water. Their bodies retain water well because the animals sweat very little in the heat.

## Conclusions

Compositions that are more than one paragraph in length usually need a short conclusion. The phrases *in conclusion* and *in summary* are sometimes used to begin a conclusion. A conclusion often restates the main idea sentence using different words. For example, in Composition 10, the main idea sentence states that although Nick and Joe are brothers, they are not similar. Notice how the conclusion restates the same idea using different words.

> *My friends cannot believe that Nick and Joe are brothers because they seem so different.*

In addition, a conclusion can summarize the major points of the composition. This summary may follow the restatement of the main idea sentence. In Composition 12, notice that the first sentence of the conclusion restates the main idea sentence. The second sentence summarizes the major points.

> *In conclusion, Paris and Washington share numerous similarities. Besides being political and tourist centers, the cities have a similar look.*

A conclusion can also make a judgment. Look at Composition 11. The conclusion includes a restatement (the first sentence) and a judgment (the second sentence).

> *The two houses for sale, then, share some similarities. However, because of the differences, the one on Duncan is a better value.*

### Exercise 12C

Write appropriate short conclusions for the compositions in Exercise 12B.

1. _____

_____

_____

_____

_____

_____

2. _____

_____

_____

_____

_____

_____

_____

3. _____

_____

_____

_____

_____

_____

_____

# GRAMMAR AND PUNCTUATION

## Comparing with *As...As*

When we compare two things that are the same, we often use *as...as*.

### EXAMPLES

Sheila is *as tall as* Jack. (They are the same height.)

Mr. Kent is *as old as* Mr. James. (They are the same age.)

### Exercise 12D

Write a comparative sentence using the information given below and the words in parentheses. *Notice that some sentences will focus on similarities, while others focus on differences.* Use a form of the verb *to be* in all your sentences.

1.   Norma and Helen are both 5 feet 8 inches (1.7 meters) tall. *(tall)*

     *Norma is as tall as Helen.*

2.   Both the Golling Falls in Austria and the Agoyan Falls in Ecuador are two hundred feet high (60 meters). *(high)*

3.   Mercury's diameter is 3,100 miles (4,960 kilometers). Jupiter's is 88,000 miles (140,800 kilometers). *(small)*

4.   Both John and Donald can lift up to 250 pounds (90 kilograms). *(strong)*

5.   The Amazon River is 4,000 miles (6,400 kilometers) long. The Nile is 4,187 miles (6,699 kilometers) long. *(long)*

6.   One cup (240 milliliters) of skim milk has 9 grams of protein. One cup of whole milk also has 9 grams of protein. *(nutritious)*

7.   Iris and Branka both weigh 130 pounds (58.5 kilograms). *(heavy)*

## Exercise 12E   Review of Comparatives

Write one or two sentences comparing or contrasting the following things. Work with a partner if you wish, and share your opinions with the class.

1.   American food, food in your country

2.   classical music, rock music

3.   speaking English, writing English

4.   you, another member of the class

5.   a computer, a human brain

6.   women, men

7.   money, love

8.   Americans, people in your country

## Showing Contrast with *Although*

Contrast can be shown by using *although* to introduce a dependent clause. The *although* clause can occur at the beginning of the sentence or at the end. Notice the difference in punctuation.

**EXAMPLES**

*Although Manhattan is a very small island,* it has a population of almost 1.5 million.

Manhattan has a population of almost 1.5 million *although it is a very small island.*

### Exercise 12F

In this exercise, you will see two sentences that express a contrast. Combine the sentences by changing the underlined sentence to a clause beginning with *although.*

1.     Violins and guitars have few things in common. Their appearance is similar.

*Violins and guitars have few things in common although their appearance is similar.*

2.     Many people are afraid of thunder. It is harmless.

3.     No one knows how the Egyptian pyramids were built. Experts have studied them for years.

4.     To most of us, a tomato is a vegetable. Botanists classify it as a fruit.

5.     The population of the world is increasing. The birth rate is falling.

6.     The United States has tried to grow tea. It has not succeeded.

Exercise 12G

Fill in the blanks with an appropriate clause beginning with *although*.

1. _Although the tuition is high_____, David will go to Harvard University.

2. They didn't turn on the air conditioner _____
_____.

3. _____, no automobile accidents were reported.

4. She bought the car _____
_____.

5. _____, I enjoyed myself at the picnic.

6. _____, she has never missed work.

7. They didn't wear coats or hats _____
_____.

8. _____,
the earthquake didn't kill anyone.

# Student Plan and Composition 12

Develop your own topic, or choose one of the following for your final comparison and contrast composition. Consider your fellow students as your audience.

1. Compare and contrast two cities or towns you know. Make your composition interesting and informative. If you want to discuss two cities or towns that are obviously different (for instance, a small town in India and a large city in the United States), it might be more interesting and informative to concentrate on the similarities. If you want to write about two cities or towns that are obviously similar (for instance, two neighboring towns on the Mediterranean), it might be more interesting to emphasize the differences.

2. Compare and contrast two members of your family. You might want to comment on some of the following points in your composition: physical appearances, personalities, attitudes and beliefs, jobs, leisure-time activities.

3. Compare and contrast yourself now with yourself five years ago. In what ways are you the same, and in what ways are you different?

4. *MORE CHALLENGING:* Now that you are familiar with the American college educational system in the United States, compare and contrast it with the system in the country you are from. In your composition, you might discuss the behavior of teachers, the behavior of students, the classroom arrangement, and homework or tests in the two countries.

## Stepping Along

**Step 1:** After choosing your topic, take time to think and write a plan of your major points and additional details. You may organize your material as in Composition 10 or as in Composition 11 or 12.

**Step 2:** Form groups of about three students. Take turns explaining your plans to one another. Stop one another and ask questions when you think something is not clear. Tell one another where you are interested in knowing additional details. (Remember that details help make your writing interesting.)

**Step 3:** Use your plan and your partners' suggestions to write your composition. Remember to use the following words to show similarity: *likewise, similarly, both, neither,* and *as . . . as.* Use these to show difference: *but, however, although, in contrast, on the other hand,* and *more/_____er than.*

**Step 4:** When you finish writing, exchange compositions with a partner. As you read your partner's composition, think about these questions.

- Is there anything in the composition that is not clear to you?

- Is there enough detail to make the composition interesting?

- Did your partner use separate paragraphs for the introduction and conclusion?

- Does the introduction prepare you for what you will read?

- Lightly underline the words that show similarity and difference. (See Step 3). Does your partner use these correctly?

- Can you give your partner any suggestions for improvement?

**Step 5:** Talk with your partner about these questions, and make suggestions for improvement.

**Step 6:** Rewrite your composition, making any changes you feel are necessary.

**Further steps:** As directed by your instructor.

# Unit 5
## *Classifying*

In this unit, you will learn how to classify. Classifying is another way to organize your thoughts and your writing. When we want to explain the relationship between *two* things, we compare and contrast them. When we want to explain the relationship among *a number* of things, we classify them. Things with similar characteristics are grouped together in this kind of organization.

Suppose you want to explain the American car market to your friend who is interested in buying an American car but knows little about what is available. You might start out by dividing cars into groups and making a chart as follows:

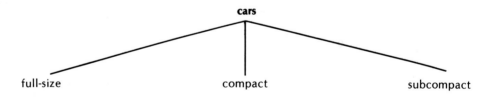

You could continue your explanation by giving examples for each group as follows:

As you make the chart, you are moving from **general** words to more **specific** words. The Ford *Crown Victoria* and the Chevrolet *Caprice* are part of the class of full-size cars. Full-size cars are part of the class of cars. Moving horizontally across the chart, we see items that are **parallel** (equal in form and content). For instance, the items *full-size cars, compact cars,* and *sub-compact cars* are similar in content and form. So are the items Ford *Crown Victoria,* Chevrolet *Caprice,* Ford *Escort,* Chevrolet *Cavalier,* Ford *Mustang,* and Chevrolet *Geo Sprint.* These are important concepts to understand when classifying. This type of chart will help you organize your thoughts before writing.

*How* we classify depends, of course, on what we want to say. In the above chart, cars are classified according to their size. They could also be classified in many other ways, including according to cost, as in the following chart.

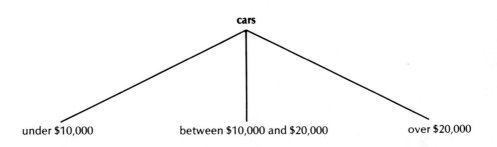

Can you think of other useful ways to classify cars?

Classification is a form of organization used in all fields when people want to understand something better or explain it to someone else. A metallurgist, for example, might find it useful to explain the properties of various metals by classifying them, and someone in the medical field might want to classify various diseases to clarify the relationship among them. What could you explain by classification in your field of interest?

# 13
# *Amount of Carbohydrates in Foods*

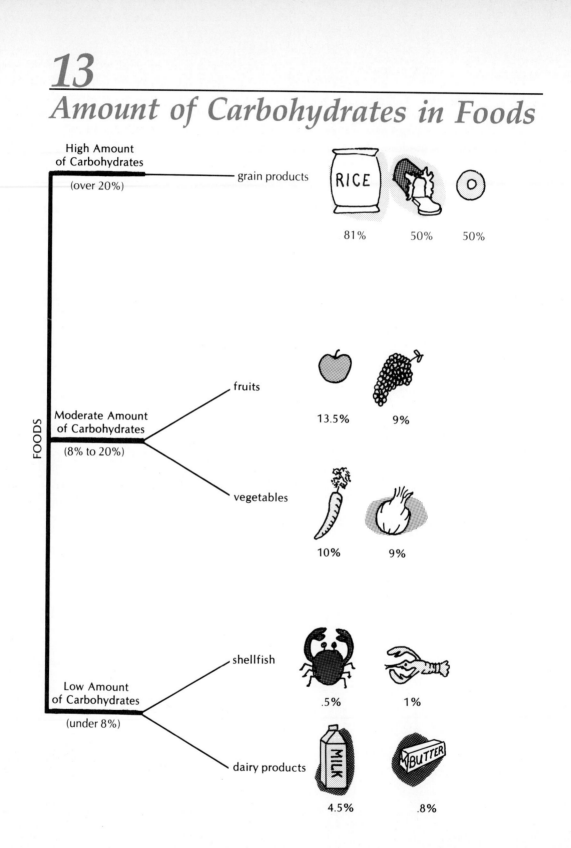

**High Amount of Carbohydrates** (over 20%) — grain products

RICE 81%   50%   50%

**Moderate Amount of Carbohydrates** (8% to 20%)

fruits   13.5%   9%

vegetables   10%   9%

**Low Amount of Carbohydrates** (under 8%)

shellfish   .5%   1%

dairy products   MILK 4.5%   BUTTER .8%

FOODS

## PLANNING

A government agency asked a nutritionist to write a pamphlet about the nutrients in various foods for the general public. Part of the pamphlet will explain the carbohydrate content of common foods. The nutritionist did some research and wrote this list.

| | | | |
|---|---|---|---|
| rice | 81% | crab | .5% |
| lobster | 1% | carrots | 10% |
| apples | 13.5% | milk | 4.5% |
| bread | 50% | doughnuts | 50% |
| onions | 9% | grapes | 9% |
| | | butter | .8% |

Then she studied her list to see how she could organize the information. She noticed that rice, bread, and doughnuts had high amounts of carbohydrate. She categorized them together (all grain products). *Look at the list below. Can you find other categories?*

| | | | |
|---|---|---|---|
| rice | 81% HIGH | crab | .5% |
| lobster | 1% | carrots | 10% |
| apples | 13.5% | milk | 4.5% |
| bread | 50% HIGH | doughnuts | 50% HIGH |
| onions | 9% | grapes | 9% |
| grain products | | butter | .8% |

Finally, the nutritionist made a detailed chart similar to the one on the opposite page. Then she felt ready to write.

## WRITING

The article appeared like this. *Underline the main idea sentence. How many paragraphs does she have? Why?*

### CARBOHYDRATES

Carbohydrates are the body's main source of energy. Many different foods include this nutrient. These foods can be classified into groups according to the amount of carbohydrates they contain.

Most grain products contain a high amount of carbohydrates, over 20 percent. Rice, for instance, is composed of 81 percent carbohydrates. Both bread and doughnuts contain 50 percent.

Fruits generally have a moderate amount of carbohydrates. Apples, for instance, are made up of 13 percent carbohydrates, and grapes contain 9 percent. Vegetables are also in the moderate group. Carrots, for example, are composed of 10 percent carbohydrates, and onions contain 9 percent.

There are two categories of food with a low amount of carbohydrates: shellfish and dairy products. Lobster and crab are examples from the shellfish group. Lobster has only .5 percent carbohydrates, and crab has 1 percent. Milk, a member of the dairy products group, contains 4.5 percent carbohydrates. Butter, another dairy product, has only .8 percent.

In summary, carbohydrates can be obtained from foods such as grain products, fruits, vegetables, shellfish, and dairy products. It is easy, therefore, to include sources of this essential nutrient in our diet.

## ORGANIZATION

Before you write, it often helps to organize your material. When you want to explain something by classifying, you can use an outline or a **classification chart.** Remember that a classification chart should move from general (at the top) to specific (at the bottom). The words placed next to each other should be parallel, or equal in form and content.

### EXAMPLES

Look back at the unit introduction for examples of classification charts.

### Exercise 13A

Find appropriate words to fill the empty boxes in the following charts.

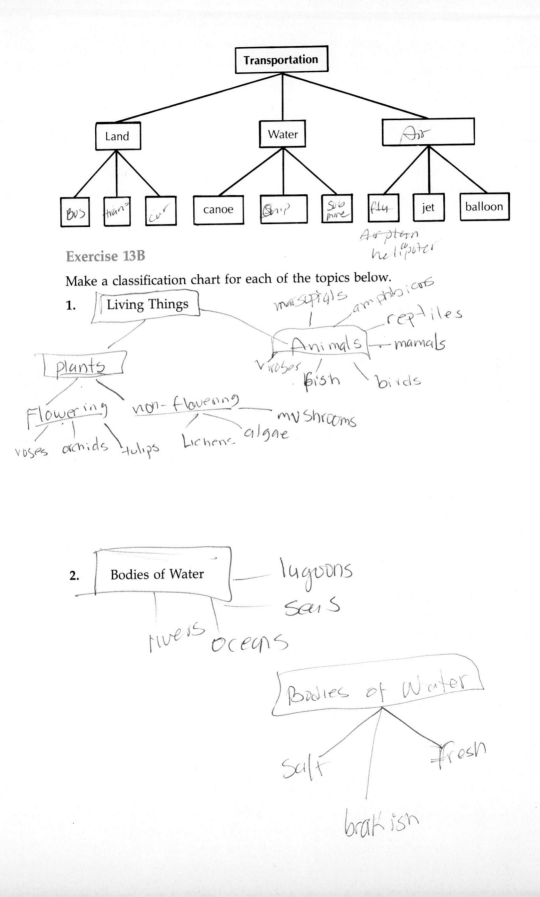

Transportation

Land | Water | Air

Bus | trans | car | canoe | ship | sub marine | fly | jet | balloon

Airplane
helicopter

## Exercise 13B

Make a classification chart for each of the topics below.

1. Living Things

plants

Animals

marsupials | amphibians | reptiles | mamals | birds | fish | viroses

Flowering | non-flowering | mushrooms

roses | orchids | tulips | Lichens | algae

2. Bodies of Water

lagoons

seas

rivers | oceans

Bodies of Water

salt | fresh

brakish

## Exercise 13C   Practice with General and Specific

In the following groups of words, one word is more specific or more general than the other words in the group. Find this word and cross it out. Then write *too specific* or *too general* in the blank.

1.
> football
> baseball
> ~~sport~~
> tennis

*too general*

2.
> ~~furniture~~
> sofa
> chair
> table

_____

3.
> dress
> coat
> ~~clothes~~
> pants

_____

4.
> fruit juices
> ~~vodka~~
> alcoholic beverages
> soft drinks

_____

5.
> vegetables
> fruit
> meat
> ~~beans~~

_____

6.
> ~~appliance~~
> dishwasher
> television
> vacuum cleaner

_____

## Exercise 13D  More Practice with General and Specific

Write a general heading for each of these categories.

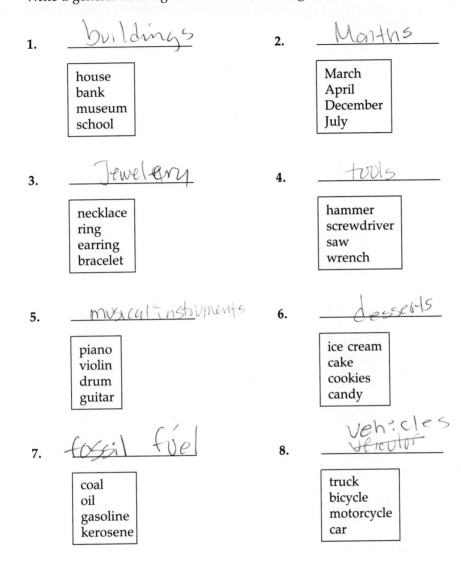

1. _buildings_

| |
|---|
| house |
| bank |
| museum |
| school |

2. _Months_

| |
|---|
| March |
| April |
| December |
| July |

3. _Jewelery_

| |
|---|
| necklace |
| ring |
| earring |
| bracelet |

4. _tools_

| |
|---|
| hammer |
| screwdriver |
| saw |
| wrench |

5. _musical instruments_

| |
|---|
| piano |
| violin |
| drum |
| guitar |

6. _desserts_

| |
|---|
| ice cream |
| cake |
| cookies |
| candy |

7. _fossil fuel_

| |
|---|
| coal |
| oil |
| gasoline |
| kerosene |

8. _vehicles_

| |
|---|
| truck |
| bicycle |
| motorcycle |
| car |

## Main Idea Sentences and Introductions

When you classify, your main idea sentence should tell the reader (1) *what* you are going to classify and (2) *how* you will divide the subject. You can mention one or more of the following:

a. number of groups
b. name of groups
c. principle of division

### EXAMPLES

*Cars* can be classified into *three major groups according to size.*

*Cars* can be classified into *three major groups: full-size, compact, and subcompact.*

*Horses* have *five major uses* in the United States.

## Exercise 13E

Circle the best main idea sentence for each of the following compositions.

1.   a. There are many different kinds of dogs in the United States.

b. Dogs have at least three major uses in American society.

c. Dogs are very popular in the United States.

Most important, dogs are pets and friends to millions of Americans. Many breeds make excellent playmates for children. Dogs make good companions and can brighten the life of an older person who lives alone.

Dogs are also widely used in hunting. Some can smell the air and locate game birds; they then guide the hunter to the proper location. Bloodhounds follow scents on the ground, and retrievers pick up birds that have been shot and bring them back to the hunter.

In addition, dogs may serve as protection. They can be trained to guard their masters' homes and bark fiercely when someone tries to enter. They also help awaken people in case of fire at night. Some dogs, known as Seeing Eye dogs, can be trained to help and protect the blind.

2.    **a.** There are many excellent Chinese dishes, including Peking duck, bird's nest soup, and Kang Pao chicken.

    **b.** Chinese food can be classified according to its nutritional value.

    **c.** Chinese food can be classified into four types: northern, coastal, inland, and southern.

Northern Chinese food is light and delicate. The staple food is wheat flour, which is used to make noodle dishes, steamed bread, and dumplings. Typical dishes from this area are barbequed meat and hot pot. The most famous northern delicacy is Peking duck.

Coastal food contains a lot of sugar and soy sauce. These are used to flavor stews, seafood, and vegetables. A well-known dish from this area is bird's nest soup.

The food from the inland area is very spicy. Small red chilies or Szechwan peppers are used liberally for seasoning and make the food taste very hot. Characteristic dishes are Szechwan beef and Kang Pao chicken.

The least greasy food is found in the southern area. Here, much of the food is stir-fried, and a lighter soy sauce is used than in the coastal area. Southern dishes are often the most costly to prepare because highly concentrated chicken broth is used. Shark's fin soup and egg rolls are typical examples of southern dishes.

3.    **a.** The United States government is divided into three branches: the executive, the legislative, and the judicial.

    **b.** The United States government includes the president, the executive departments, the Congress, and the Supreme Court.

    **c.** The executive, the legislative, and the judicial branches are the three major parts of the government.

The executive branch of the government consists of the executive office of the president, the executive departments, and the independent agencies. The president is the chief executive and is elected by the people. The executive departments, such as state, treasury, defense, and labor, conduct the administration of the national government. The independent agencies deal with areas such as aeronautics and space and interstate commerce.

The legislative branch consists of the Congress and five administrative agencies. Congress is divided into the Senate and the House of Representatives. The Senate has 100 senators, two from every state. The population of each state determines how many representatives it has in the House of Representatives.

The judicial branch includes the entire federal court system. These courts decide cases that involve the Constitution and federal laws. The highest court in the United States is the Supreme Court. The president appoints its justices, who hold office for life.

### Exercise 13F

Write an introduction for each of the three compositions in Exercise 13E. Begin your introduction with a common belief or general statement. Then continue with the main idea sentence you have chosen.

1. _____

_____

_____

_____

_____

_____

_____

2. _____

_____

_____

_____

_____

_____

3. _____

_____

_____

_____

_____

_____

## Transitions for Giving Examples

When you classify, you divide your subject into groups or categories. For each category you mention, you should give examples. Your writing will be easier to understand if you use transitions to introduce your examples. The first example you give may be introduced by *for example* or *for instance*. Further examples may be introduced by *also* or *another*, both of which indicate addition.

### Exercise 13G

Look back at Composition 13. Circle examples of the above transitions. Notice how each is used.

### Exercise 13H

The following is the introduction and the first paragraph of a composition that classifies recent American films. Fill in the blanks with appropriate transitions.

> The American film industry is constantly releasing new films on a variety of subjects. Most of these films, however, can be divided into six general categories.
>
> Science-fiction films are one popular type of film. *Star Wars*, _____, tells a futuristic tale about a civil war between planets in an imaginary galaxy. *2001: A Space Odyssey* is _____ a science-fiction film. It is about two astronauts and a computer on a space voyage to Jupiter. _____ well-known science-fiction film is *Close Encounters of the Third Kind*. In this film, aliens from outer space come down to earth and appear to humans.

Exercise 13I

Put the following information in paragraph form. Use appropriate transitions. Your paragraph will be the second paragraph of the composition in 13H.

> Disaster films, especially popular in the 1970s, are a second type of American film. *Jaws* is a 1970s disaster movie that tells the story of a shark that repeatedly attacks people.
>
> A popular film of this decade, *Earthquake,* shows the city of Los Angeles being destroyed by an earthquake.
>
> *Towering Inferno* is a disaster film. In this movie, a fire breaks out in a skyscraper, and many people are burned to death or die by jumping out of windows.

_____

_____

_____

_____

_____

_____

_____

_____

_____

_____

_____

## GRAMMAR AND PUNCTUATION

### The Colon

A colon (:) is often used to introduce a list or series of items. The part of the sentence *after* the colon explains or gives details about what appears in the part of the sentence *before* the colon. When the word in front of the series is a verb or a preposition, a colon is not used. However, if the word in front of the series is a noun, you must use the colon.

#### EXAMPLES

*Colon used:*       They visited four *cities:* New York, London, Paris, and Istanbul.

*No colon used:*   They visited New York, London, Paris, and Istanbul.

*Colon used:*       There are two categories of food in the low-carbohydrate *group:* shellfish and dairy products.

*No colon used:*   The two categories of food in the low-carbohydrate group are shellfish and dairy products.

### Exercise 13J

Put a colon where appropriate in the following sentences. Some sentences need no colon.

1.    The arts can be divided into three groups: performing arts, visual arts, and literature.

2.    The four national languages in Switzerland are German, French, Italian, and Romansh.

3.    The human nervous system has three main divisions the central nervous system, the peripheral nervous system, and the autonomic nervous system.

4.    Books can be classified into two groups fiction and nonfiction.

5.    To play baseball, you need a bat, a baseball, and a glove.

6.    New York has five boroughs Manhattan, Queens, Brooklyn, the Bronx, and Richmond.

7.    John applied to four schools the University of Michigan, Columbia University, the University of Pennsylvania, and the University of Colorado.

8.    The blood of all higher animals consists of plasma, red blood cells, white blood cells, and blood platelets.

9.    The flight departure times will be 8:15, 9:20, 11:45, and 6:15.

10.   There are five principal types of dams earth dams, rock-fill dams, gravity dams, arch dams, and buttress dams.

11.   Yugoslavia has six republics Slovenia, Croatia, Serbia, Bosnia and Herzegovina, Montenegro, and Macedonia.

12.   A snow skier needs the following equipment skis, boots, and poles.

# Student Plan 13
## Amount of Protein in Foods

Suppose you work for a health organization, and you have been asked to classify and explain sources of protein in a handbook for the general public. With a partner or in a small group, use the information below to complete the classification chart and write a main idea sentence.

rice — 6.5%
mushrooms — 2%
beef — 27%
bananas — 1.3%

cherries — .8%
cottage cheese — 13.5%
bread — 8.8%

chicken — 31.7%
broccoli — 3%
cheese — 25%

**Main idea sentence\*** _____

_____

_____

\*You may want to write your main idea sentence after you finish the plan.

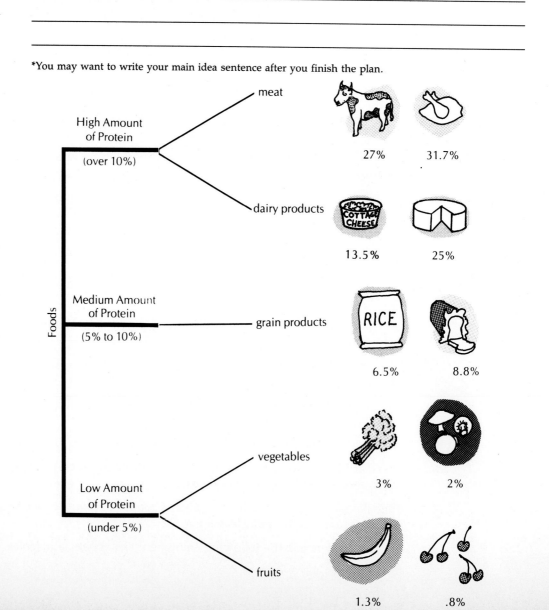

Foods

High Amount of Protein (over 10%)

meat

27%    31.7%

dairy products

13.5%    25%

Medium Amount of Protein (5% to 10%)

grain products

RICE

6.5%    8.8%

Low Amount of Protein (under 5%)

vegetables

3%    2%

fruits

1.3%    .8%

# Student Composition 13
## Amount of Protein in Foods

**Stepping Along**

**Step 1:** Use your chart to help you write a composition. In addition to your major paragraphs, write an introduction using your main idea sentence, and write a conclusion. Use appropriate transitions.

**Step 2:** Exchange compositions with a partner. As you read your partner's composition, think about these questions.

- Has your partner used the correct number of paragraphs?

- Does your partner state the general topic at the beginning of the paragraph and then move to specific details?

- Has your partner used transitions to introduce some of the examples?

- Can you give your partner any suggestions for improvement?

**Step 3:** Talk with your partner about your compositions. Try to agree on improvements you can make.

**Step 4:** Rewrite your composition, making any changes you feel are necessary.

**Further steps:** As directed by your instructor.

# 14
## *Contact Sports*

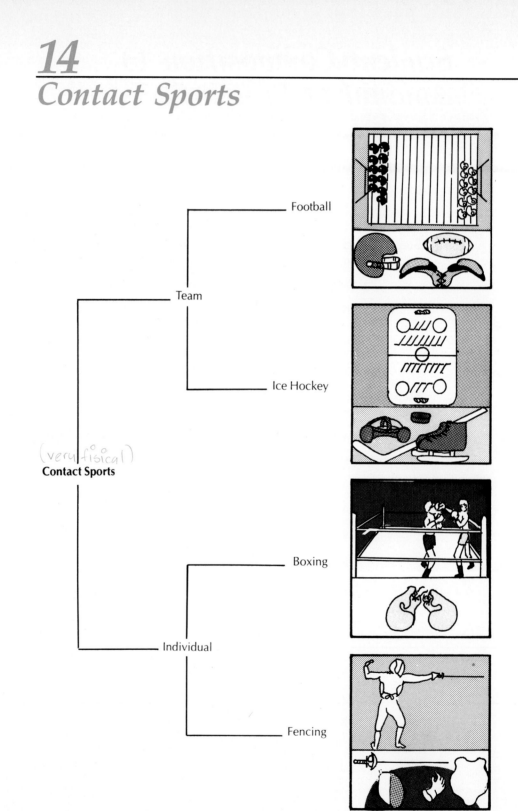

Football

Team

Ice Hockey

(very fisical)
**Contact Sports**

Boxing

Individual

Fencing

## PLANNING

An encyclopedia for children wanted to include a short entry explaining contact sports and giving some examples. The writer of the article decided he could divide contact sports into two categories. *How did he divide them? What examples of specific sports did he give? What other information did he include?*

> (Team) contact sports:
>   football - 11 players, field, helmets,
>       shoulder pads, football
>   ice hockey - 6 players, ice rink, skates,
>       helmets, hockey sticks, puck
> (Individual) contact sports:
>   boxing - boxing ring, gloves
>   fencing - no special place, mask,
>       foil, heavy clothing

Colon
: a list will follow.

ThS
Large group → group / smaller sub-groups

## WRITING

The finished entry looks like this. *How many paragraphs are there? What does each one cover? Underline the main idea sentence and circle the transitions that introduce examples.*

### Contact Sports

Many sports require physical contact between opponents as part of the play. These contact sports can be divided into two groups: team and individual.

One of the most popular team contact sports in the United States is football. There are eleven players on each team, and the game is played outside on a field called a gridiron. The players wear helmets and shoulder pads for protection and use an oval leather football! Another popular team contact sport is ice hockey. Each team has six players. The game is played on an ice-covered rink. Hockey players wear ice skates, of course, and helmets for protection. They use a curved stick to hit a rubber disk called a *puck*.

Individual contact sports also exist. One example is boxing. Matches are held in a boxing ring—a small, roped-off area. Boxers use thick leather gloves to punch their opponents. Fencing also falls into this category. This sport requires no special location, but fencers need a sword called a *foil*, a mask, and heavy clothing.

In summary, contact sports are of two types. There are team contact sports, such as football and ice hockey, and individual contact sports, such as boxing and fencing.

## ORGANIZATION

### Exercise 14A    Classification Charts and Outlines

When people classify things, some like to make charts first, and some prefer the traditional outline. Notice how the following words can be organized either in a chart or an outline.

Minerals
/\
Iron   Gold

Plants
/\
Oak tree  Fern

Animals
/\
Dogs   Camels

I. Minerals
    A. Iron
    B. Gold
II. Plants
    A. Oak tree
    B. Fern
III. Animals
    A. Dogs
    B. Camels

Now organize the following sets of words either with a chart *or* an outline.

South America
Switzerland
Ethiopia
Africa
France
United States
North America
Nigeria
Europe
Kenya
Germany
Argentina
Bolivia
Canada
Chile

Africa    South    America
Ethiopia      Argentina —
Nigeria       Bolivia
Kenya          Chile

North America  Europe
   U.S.A         Switzerland
   Canada        France
                 Germany

duck  palomas
beef
fish
chicken
poultry
tuna
lamb
swordfish
pork
meat
turkey

meat          fish          Poultry
beef        swordfish       chicken
chicken       tuna          turkey
pork                         duck
lamb
poultry

I meat
   A
   B
   C
II poultry
   A
   B
   C
IV fish
   A
   B
   C

Exercise 14B   Irrelevant Sentences

Find the irrelevant sentence in each of the following classification paragraphs, and cross it out.

1.          Gardeners classify flowering plants into three groups: annuals, biennials, and perennials. Annuals normally live only one year. Examples of annuals are cornflowers and marigolds. It is expensive to use annuals in your garden because you must replace them every year. Biennials live for two years after the seeds are planted and bloom well only in the second year. Common biennials are foxgloves and hollyhocks. Perennials may live for many years. The flowers begin blooming the year after they are planted. Perennials include roses and violets.

2.          The field of engineering can be divided into several different areas. Civil engineering is the branch that involves the construction of roads, bridges, railroads, and canals. Canals vary in length and width. Mechanical engineering deals with the designs and materials that are used in the construction of various kinds of machinery. Electrical engineering deals with the generation and transmission of electrical energy. Other areas of engineering include chemical, biomedical, aeronautical, and military engineering.

3.          There are three types of gliders: the primary glider, the utility glider, and the sailplane. The primary glider has an open body, so the pilot has no protection. It is used for coasting downhill. The utility glider, which has an enclosed body, gives the occupants good protection. It is used for training in soaring and gliding. The sailplane has a slender body. It makes the best use of air currents and is used for soaring. The first World Championship Soaring Competition was held in Sweden in 1950.

# GRAMMAR AND PUNCTUATION

## Passive Sentences

All the sentences you have written so far in this text have been active sentences. An **active sentence** is a sentence in which the **agent** (that is, the one who performs the action) is in subject position. Sometimes, we do not know who the agent is, or we do not think that the agent is particularly important. We can then write a **passive sentence** by moving the agent out of the subject position and making the **receiver** the subject.

Active sentences in the present tense can be changed to passive sentences by making the receiver the subject and by using the present form of *to be + a past participle*. Note the following examples.

### EXAMPLES

1a. *Active:*      Someone repairs *the roads* every year.

  b. *Passive:*      *The roads* are repaired every year.

2a. *Active:*      Americans play *baseball* in the summer.

  b. *Passive:*      *Baseball* is played (by Americans) in the summer.

In sentence 1b, the agent (*someone*) has been omitted because it is unknown or unimportant. In sentence 2b, the agent (*Americans*) may or may not be included, depending on its importance.

## Exercise 14C

Change the following active sentences to passive sentences. If the subject of the active sentence is *someone* or *people,* drop it when changing to the passive.

1.    Golfers use clubs.

    *Clubs are used by golfers.*

2.    People all over the world study English.

3.    People play tennis and volleyball on courts.

4.    Few Americans speak Arabic.

5.     People make paper from wood.

6.     People buy medicines at the drugstore.

7.     The government collects taxes every year.

8.     The landlord furnishes the apartment.

9.     Someone serves lunch at noon.

10.     Someone cleans the rooms once a week.

11.     A mechanic on Green Street fixes my car.

12.     Someone delivers the mail in the afternoon.

Exercise 14D   Punctuation: Review of the Colon

Summarize the information in each group of sentences by organizing it into one sentence with a colon. Don't forget to use commas between items.

1.   To wash and wax a car, you need several things. First, you need a bucket of water, a sponge, and some mild detergent. After you wash the car, you need some wax and a soft cloth.

*To wash and wax a car, you need several things: a bucket of water, a sponge, some mild detergent, some wax, and a soft cloth.*

2.   Sam visited several countries on his vacation. First, he toured Spain. Then he went to France and Germany. He also stopped in England and went through Nova Scotia on his way home.

*Sam visited several countries on his vacation: Spain, France, Germany, England, and Nova Scotia.*

3.   Frank bought a lot of ingredients for his casserole. He bought noodles and a can of tomato sauce. He also bought mozzarella cheese and a pound of ground beef.

4.   The new movie will be shown at the theater at various times. You can see it in the afternoon at 3:15 and 5:15. If you want to go at night, you can see the movie at 7:15 and 9:15.

*The new movie will be shown at the theater at various times: in the afternoon 3:5*

5.   Juanita is considering several possibilities for a career. She likes law. She is also interested in medicine. In addition, she is considering teaching.

# Student Plan 14
## Careers and Noncontact Sports

A. What field of study do you plan to pursue at the university? Do you know what careers are available in that field? Classify and explain them. Put down your ideas first in chart or outline form.

OR

B. Imagine that you want to explain something about noncontact sports to someone who knows little about sports.

Discuss the pictures below with a partner or a small group. Decide on the best way to classify the sports (look back at the chart on page 170 if you need help). Add examples of other noncontact sports if you can, and make a chart or an outline.

**Volleyball**

volleyball court
volleyball
net

**Snow Skiing**

skis
poles
boots

**Bobsledding**

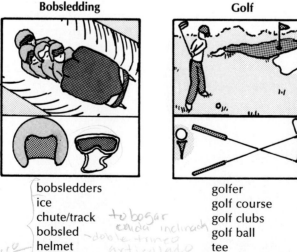

bobsledders
ice
chute/track    ~~to bogar~~
                ~~caida inclinada~~
bobsled  ~~-doble trineo~~
helmet   ~~articulado~~
goggles

~~casco~~

~~Lentes~~
~~de~~
~~camino~~

**Golf**

golfer
golf course
golf clubs
golf ball
tee

178

*Main idea sentence\** _____

_____

_____

_____

_____

_____

*You may want to write your main idea sentence after you finish the plan.

## Make Your Chart or Outline Here

# Student Composition 14
## Careers and Noncontact Sports

### Stepping Along

**Step 1:** Use your chart or outline to help you write a composition. In addition to your major paragraphs, write an introduction using your main idea sentence, and write a conclusion. Use appropriate transitions.

**Step 2:** Exchange compositions with a partner. As you read your partner's composition, think about these questions.

- Is everything in your partner's composition clear to you?

- Can you give your partner three suggestions for improvement?

**Step 3:** Talk with your partner about your compositions. Try to agree on improvements you can make.

**Step 4:** Rewrite your composition, making any changes you feel are necessary.

**Further steps:** As directed by your instructor.

# 15
## The Uses of Cattle

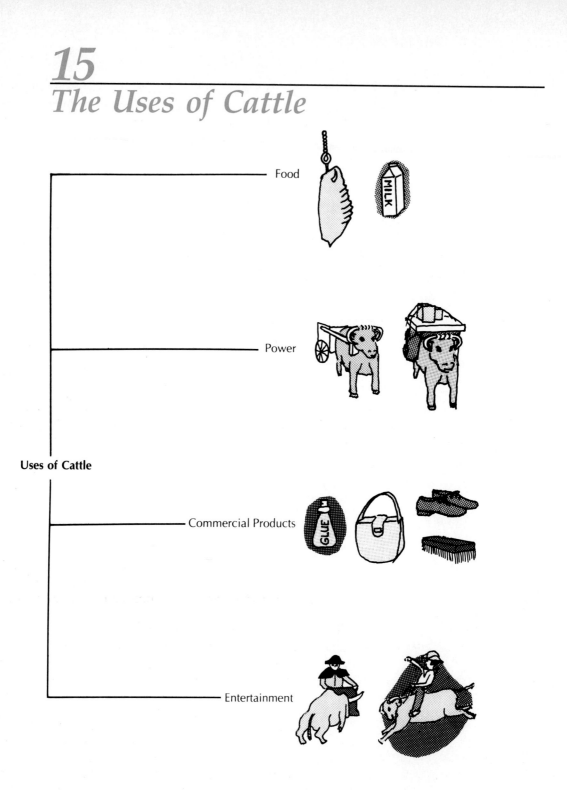

Uses of Cattle

Food

Power

Commercial Products

Entertainment

## PLANNING

In a Future Farmers of America club in a high school, the members were each asked to research and write a short paper on the different uses of farm animals around the world. One student chose *cattle.* She went to the library and found these uses of cattle.

- beef and veal
- glue made from bones
- milk
- rodeos in the U.S.
- to pull plows and carts in Europe, Africa, Asia
- bullfighting in Mexico, Venezuela, Spain
- blankets, carpets, brushes (from cow hair)
- leather bags and shoes (from cow hide)
- as pack animals in Senegal and Chad

Then she tried to classify the uses. Can *you* see any categories? Study her notes.
Eventually, she decided to classify the uses of cattle into the four categories on the opposite page. Do any of her categories match yours?

## WRITING

This is what the student finally wrote.

### The Uses of Cattle

Cattle are important animals in many parts of the world, and people use them in a variety of ways. These uses can be classified into four major categories: food, power, commercial products, and entertainment.

First of all, cattle are very important for the world's food supply. Over 50 percent of the meat we eat is beef or veal. Cattle also supply 95 percent of the world's milk.

In addition, cattle are an important source of power, especially in less-developed countries. They are used in agriculture to pull plows and carts in parts of central Europe, Africa, and Asia. In countries such as Senegal and Chad, cattle serve as pack animals.

The third major use of cattle is for various commercial products. For instance, glue is made from their bones, and leather goods such as bags and shoes are made from their hides. Cow hair is used in some blankets, carpets, and brushes.

Finally, cattle can provide us with entertainment. A savage breed of cattle is used for bullfighting in countries such as Spain, Mexico, and Venezuela. Cattle also play an important role in the rodeo, a popular spectator sport in the western half of the United States.

These, then, are the four major uses of cattle. We can see why these animals have such importance in many areas of the world.

# ORGANIZATION

### Exercise 15A    Classification Charts

Look at the following names.

*President* John F. Kennedy     *President* George Washington

*President* General Charles de Gaulle   *President* Mao Tse-tung

*Queen* Queen Victoria     *writer* Fyodor Dostoyevsky

*Autor/Writer* Ernest Hemingway    *Pres* Abraham Lincoln

*Writer* Charles Dickens    *writer* Gabriel Garcia Marquez

*writer* Mark Twain    *writer* Johann von Goethe

*King* Louis XVI

There are several different ways in which these people can be classified. One way is to classify them according to the century in which they achieved worldwide fame. The classification chart would then look like this.

With the help of your classmates and your instructor, think of one or two other ways to classify the names, and make the charts in the space below.

*Vocation*

*political leaders - writers*

## Exercise 15B    Main Idea Sentences and Introductions

Write an introduction for each of the following classification compositions. Remember that your main idea sentence should tell the reader *what* you are going to classify and *how* you will divide your subject.

1. _____

_____

_____

_____

_____

_____

*caracol*

Land snails live in damp, shady places under logs and stones; at the edges of ponds and rivers; and in woods. In tropical forests, some even live in trees. Most land snails use lungs to breathe.

Freshwater snails live in rivers, ponds, lakes, and hot springs. Some kinds have lungs and must come to the surface of the water to breathe oxygen from the air. Others have gills, which take oxygen directly from the water.

Saltwater, or marine, snails are the largest group of snails. Some types live along the seashore, and others live on the ocean floor. Most marine snails have gills.

*Ths: There are three kinds of snails: land, freshwater and marine.*
*snails live in (land) (fresh water) and marine habitats*
*there*

2. _____

_____

_____

_____

*Pearls are produced by oysters alone,*
*by oysters with human help and by humans.*

Natural pearls are the most valuable kind of pearls. They are produced when a grain of sand or a tiny animal enters an oyster's shell. Gradually, the oyster completely covers it with layers of a substance called nacre.

Cultured pearls are real pearls that are made by oysters but with human help. A small mother-of-pearl bead is placed in the oyster's shell. The finished pearl has fewer but thicker layers of nacre than the natural pearl.

Imitation pearls are the last type of pearl and are made entirely by humans. Manufacturers coat glass beads with pearl essence. This is a creamy liquid that is extracted from fish scales.

*There are three different kinds of pearls:*
*natural, cultured and imitation.*

**3.**  ⟶ There are three kinds of cloth:
animal, plant, and synthetic.

⟶ Fibers come from natural animal, plant, and synthetic sources.

_____

_____

_____

Some kinds of cloth are made from fibers obtained from animals. For example, wool comes from the fleece of certain kinds of sheep. It is a warm fabric and a natural insulator. Silk is made from fibers that are spun by silkworms. It is a light but warm fabric.

Other fabrics are made from plant fibers. Fibers from the cotton plant are spun into cotton cloth. The resulting fabric is light and comfortable. Linen also comes from plants. It is thicker than cotton and is made from the fibers of the flax plant.

Synthetics, fabrics that are not from animals or plants, are made by humans. They are usually cheaper and easier to care for than natural fabrics. Orlon, for example, resembles wool but is easily washable. It is made from a chemical. Dacron, which resists fading and wrinkling, is made from coal, water, limestone, and natural gases.

develop an introduction

1. — Challenge a popular idea or belief.
2. — General information
3. — bisic question
4. — telling story

Exercise 15C   Conclusions

Add a one-sentence conclusion to each of the short compositions in Exercise 15B.

1.  _____

_____

_____

_____

_____

_____

2.  _____

_____

_____

_____

_____

_____

3.  _____

_____

_____

_____

_____

_____

## Exercise 15D   Review of Transition

The following composition does not read smoothly because it contains no transitions in the major paragraphs. Rewrite it, using appropriate transitions.

There are thousands of different diseases in the world, and new ones are discovered all the time. However, they can all be classified into two categories: infectious and noninfectious.

Infectious diseases are caused by bacteria or viruses. They can be passed from person to person by close contact. The common cold and influenza are infectious diseases. Tuberculosis, a lung malady, is an infectious disease. AIDS is one of the most serious infectious diseases of our time.

Noninfectious diseases are usually caused by bodily malfunction or a genetic problem. They cannot be transmitted from one person to another. Heart disease is a noninfectious disease that is becoming common for both men and women. A noninfectious disease is cystic fibrosis. It strikes young children and is usually fatal.

Scientists continue to discover new diseases. Any new disease, however, is still classified as either infectious or noninfectious.

*Rewritten Composition*

_____

_____

_____

_____

_____

_____

_____

_____

_____

_____

_____

_____

_____

_____

_____

_____

_____

_____

## Giving Examples with *Such As*

You have learned that when you give examples, you can use the transitions *for example, for instance, also,* and *another.* If you wish to list your examples as briefly as possible, you can use *such as* + your specific examples immediately following your general word or phrase.

**EXAMPLE**

Cattle *also* frequently serve as pack animals in countries *such as* Chad and Senegal.

Find additional examples in the composition on page 183.

### Exercise 15E

Read the following groups of sentences. Combine each group into one sentence using *such as.* Omit *some* in your new sentence.

1.  Some parts of the world remain virtually unexplored. For instance, the Arctic and Antarctica have not been explored much. Neither have the Himalayas or the Amazon Basin.

    *Parts of the world such as the Arctic, Antarctica, the Himalayas, and the Amazon Basin remain virtually unexplored.*

2.  Some birds cannot fly. For instance, penguins cannot fly. Neither can ostriches.

3.  Some athletes are internationally known. The soccer player Maradona and the boxer Muhammad Ali are both famous around the world.

4.  Some countries have more than one official language. For example, Switzerland has more than one official language. So do Norway and Yugoslavia.

5.  In the twentieth century, some presidents were elected to the White House more than once. Franklin Roosevelt was elected four times, for example. Ronald Reagan, Richard Nixon, and Woodrow Wilson were each elected twice.

# GRAMMAR AND PUNCTUATION

### Exercise 15F   Review of Punctuation

Punctuate these sentences correctly.

1. Although Beethoven became totally deaf at age forty-six he continued writing great music.

2. The helicopter for instance is one type of motorized aircraft.

3. The United States armed forces are divided into four groups the army the navy the air force and the marines.

4. She doesn't read English however she speaks it very well.

5. The world's oil supply is shrinking so oil is increasing in value.

6. After they went to New York City they visited Peoria Illinois.

7. Scientists are interested in the theory of black holes because it may explain the origin of the universe.

8. On April 4 1968 Martin Luther King, Jr. was fatally shot in Memphis Tennessee.

9. Jupiter the largest planet has a diameter of 88000 miles.

10. Bamboo is used for two purposes for food and for commercial products.

11. The Venus flytrap a plant that eats flies and other insects lives in coastal areas.

12. The five largest countries in the world are the Soviet Union Canada the People's Republic of China the United States and Brazil.

# Student Plan and Composition 15

Develop your own topic, or choose one of the topics below for your final classification composition. Consider your fellow students as your audience.

1. Choose an animal that is used for several different purposes and classify its uses. Horses, camels, elephants, llamas, and goats are just some of the animals that are used in a variety of ways. The major categories in your composition may be somewhat different from those in Composition 15. For example, you may need to include *transportation* as a category. When you give examples for each use of the animal, be as specific as possible. You can mention, for instance, *where* the animal is used for a specific purpose, *how widespread* the use is, or *why* the animal is used in a particular way. You may wish to look in an encyclopedia for more information about your animal.

2. Explain the various holidays you celebrate in your country by classifying them.

3. Explain a topic in your major field by classifying it. For example, if your field is computer science, you might attempt to classify computers or computer software.

4. *MORE CHALLENGING:* Think of all the methods you have used to improve your English or those you have heard of or would like to try. Explain these methods by classifying them.

## Stepping Along

**Step 1:** After choosing your topic, brainstorm with other students who have chosen the same topic. You should write down any ideas that occur to you (in any order). For topic 1, write down as many uses of the animal as you can think of. For topic 2, write down names of holidays, and for topic 4, various methods of learning English.

**Step 2:** Individually or in groups, organize your material by putting it in a classification chart or an outline. Think of a general heading for each of your groups.

**Step 3:** On your own, write a composition using your chart or outline. Remember to write an introduction and conclusion, and use appropriate transitions.

**Step 4:** Exchange compositions with someone you didn't work with on Steps 1 or 2. As you read your partner's composition, think about these questions.

- Is the introduction interesting?
- Are the general categories of the classification clear to you?
- Does your partner support each category with clear examples?
- Are transitions used appropriately?
- Can you give your partner any suggestions for improvement?

**Step 5:** Talk with your partner about the strong and weak points of your compositions.

**Step 6:** Rewrite your composition, making any changes you feel are necessary.

# Unit 6

## Describing a Mechanism or a Process

When you describe a mechanism or a process, you explain how something works or takes place by analyzing its parts or elements and then examining their relationship to one another. For example, you can explain how a barometer measures the pressure of the air by identifying its parts—a reservoir, mercury, a glass tube, and a scale—and then explaining how they function together. Or you can explain how the respiratory system works by analyzing what the diaphragm, nasal cavity, trachea, bronchial tubes, and lungs do so that we can breathe. There are several important things to remember when you explain a mechanism or a process.

1. *Be sure to include all major parts or elements.*
   Each major part or element has a particular function and contributes to make the mechanism or process work. Therefore, do not leave out any major part or element.

2. *Identify each part or element.*
   You can help your audience visualize each part or element by giving at least one of the following pieces of information: a description, the location, and/or the function. This applies mainly to mechanisms.

3. *Follow chronological order.*
   Chronological order is important when you explain how the parts or elements work together. For example, when describing how plants and animals become petrified, it is necessary to follow a certain order: (1) water dissolves away the original substance of the plant or animal, and (2) minerals replace the dissolved substance. If you don't follow this order, the process of petrification will not be clear to the reader.

4. *Use accurate terminology.*

You will often need to use technical terminology to name a part, a process, or a function. When this is necessary, do so. Don't, for instance, call one of the parts of a camera "a device that controls the amount of light that enters the lens." Call that device by its name, *shutter.* You may find the right terminology in dictionaries, encyclopedias, or textbooks.

5. *Keep your audience in mind.*

You must decide whom you are writing for. For instance, your explanation of how a pacemaker works will be different depending on whether it is given to a medical student or to a general audience. In this unit, your writing will be geared to a very general audience. However, when you explain a mechanism or process to a specialized audience, the same principles apply.

People in different fields make use of this kind of organization when they write. A dental student, for example, may need to describe the process of tooth decay, or a nuclear engineer may want to explain how a nuclear reactor works.

# 16
## A Television

**The Parts**

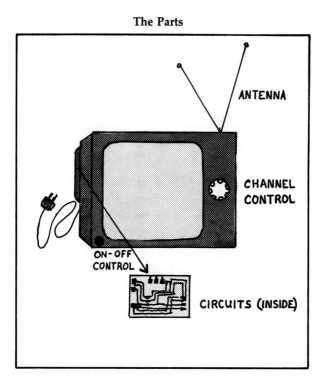

ANTENNA

CHANNEL CONTROL

ON-OFF CONTROL

CIRCUITS (INSIDE)

**How They Work**

## PLANNING

A student in a basic electronics course was asked to write a short description of an electrical appliance for a general audience. She chose to write about a television. First, she made an idea map of the parts of a TV, and then she made notes about how the parts work together.

I) cord with **body** circuits
plug — (The Parts)
— screen
antenna
Controls
on-off  channel-changing

II) How They Work
A. Plug goes into socket
B. On-off control to ON
C. Circuits → picture → screen
D. Channel control to proper channel
E. Antenna → clearer picture

## WRITING

Here is her final draft. *How is it different from her plan? Underline the main idea sentence.*

### A Television

Televisions can be as large as a home movie screen or as small as a hand. They can be color or black-and-white. However, all televisions have the same basic parts: a body, circuits, a screen, various controls, an antenna, and a cord with a plug.

First, there is a box-shaped body. Inside the body are complex circuits, which amplify and separate the video and audio signals. Next is the glass screen where the picture appears. There are also two major controls. One is the on-off control, which also alters the volume, and the other is the control that changes the channels. The antenna—a long, thin rod on the top of the set—improves the reception. Finally, there is the cord with a plug, which is plugged into a socket in the wall.

The parts work together as follows: First, the plug must be plugged into the socket, and the on-off control must be turned on. The circuits then send the picture to the screen. The channel control can be turned to choose a channel. If the picture is not clear, the antenna can be moved.

In summary, there are different sizes and types of televisions, but all have the same basic parts.

## ORGANIZATION

### Main Idea Sentences and Introductions

When you describe a mechanism or a process, your main idea sentence should (1) name the mechanism or process, (2) either name the parts or elements or tell how many there are, and (3) possibly mention how or where the mechanism is used or when the process occurs.

#### EXAMPLES

Note how the following examples show the above points.

There are many kinds of watches, but most have gears, a face, hands, a stem, and a watchband.

In order for plants to make food, several elements must play a role: air, light, stomata, water, roots, and chloroplasts.

The eye is a complex mechanism that can be better understood when its eight major parts are analyzed.

The stapler, a necessary tool in any office, is composed of six major parts.

Exercise 16A

Read the following short compositions carefully. Each describes a mechanism. Circle the best main idea sentence for each.

1.  **a.** Each pair of scissors has the same three basic parts.

    **b.** To use a pair of scissors, follow these simple steps.

    **c.** The mechanism I want to talk about has three basic parts.

First are the sharp cutting blades, which are made of steel. These cutting blades are joined in the middle by a small pivot pin similar to a small screw. On top of the blades are round or oval handles, which provide openings for the thumb and first finger.

When the handles are pressed together with the thumb and first finger, the sharp blades meet and cut the material between the blades.

2.  **a.** An electric beater makes cooking easy and works like this.

    **b.** An electric beater is composed of a body, a motor, a handle, a switch, two beaters, and a cord with a plug.

    **c.** An electric beater has three basic parts: the body, the handle, and the switch.

The body of the electric beater is usually made of strong plastic and holds the motor. The handle, located on top of the body, makes the beater easy to hold. On the handle is the switch. It turns the motor on or off and controls the rotation speed of the beaters. The two oval-shaped beaters, which are made of strips of metal, are inserted into two holes in the underside of the body. Finally, there is the cord with a plug, which must be inserted into a wall socket.

A beater works like this. When the cord is plugged into the wall, the switch can be turned on. The motor then begins to run. The motor activates the beaters, which begin to rotate. Now the beater is ready to beat the eggs.

3.  **a.** Riding a bicycle, a popular form of recreation, is not difficult if you keep all of the bicycle parts in working order.

    **b.** All bicycles consist of these major parts: the frame, the wheels, the pedals, the chain, the seat, and the handlebars.

    **c.** The frame, the wheels, and the pedals are very important parts of the bicycle.

The frame of the bicycle is made of light metal and is triangular in shape. It is mounted on top of the two wheels. The pedals are square pieces, which are usually made of metal. These pedals are attached to a chain mechanism that drives the rear wheel. The handlebars, made for the hands to hold, are attached to the front wheel and control the steering. The seat, where the cyclist sits, is the triangular leather piece on the top of the frame.

The parts work together in this way: The cyclist sits on the seat and pushes the pedals. The chain then begins to turn and drives the rear wheel. Once the bicycle is in motion, it can be steered by moving the handlebars right or left.

### Exercise 16B

Write an introduction for each of the three compositions in Exercise 16A. Begin your introduction with a general statement. Then continue with the main idea sentence you have chosen. You may have to make some small changes in your main idea sentence.

1. _____

_____

_____

_____

_____

_____

2. _____

_____

_____

_____

_____

_____

3. _____

_____

_____

_____

_____

_____

## Identifying the Parts of a Mechanism

When you describe a mechanism, it is necessary to name all the major parts. You should also **identify** each part. You can identify a part by giving one or more of the following pieces of information: the *location* of the part, a *description* of the part, or the *function* of the part.

### EXAMPLE

The following example from the composition on page 197 gives all three pieces of information about a television antenna.

The antenna—a long, thin rod (*description*) on the top of the set (*location*)—improves the reception (*function*).

## Exercise 16C

Look back at Composition 16. Tell which pieces of information (*location*, *description*, *function*) are given for each part.

## Exercise 16D

Look at the following pictures. Give the *location*, a *description*, and the *function* for each of the indicated parts. You will need the help of your dictionary or your instructor for some vocabulary items.

1.

STEMS

Location: *attached to the lenses*

_____

Description: *thin metal and/or plastic pieces*

Function: *They hook on the ears and hold the glasses in place.*

2.

BUMPERS

Location: _____

_____

Description: _____

_____

Function: _____

_____

3.

SOFT DRINK CAP

Cola

Location: _____

_____

Description: _____

_____

Function: _____

_____

4.

WATCHBAND

Location: _____

_____

Description: _____

_____

Function: _____

_____

5.

SHOELACES

Location: _____

_____

Description: _____

_____

Function: _____

_____

## GRAMMAR AND PUNCTUATION

### Relative Clauses: Nonrestrictive

In this unit, you will practice writing a grammatical structure that is very useful for describing mechanisms and processes. Look at the two sentences below.

> The body contains complex circuits. These circuits amplify and separate the video and audio signals.

The second sentence repeats a noun from the first sentence. We can join the two sentences by dropping the second noun and substituting *which* (or *who* when referring to people). The part of the sentence that begins with *which* or *who* is called a **relative clause.** This clause must be placed immediately after the noun or noun phrase it modifies, as in the examples below. Notice the punctuation.

> *which*
> The body contains complex circuits. These ~~circuits~~ amplify and separate the video and audio signals.
>
> The body contains complex circuits, *which amplify and separate the video and audio signals.*

Notice how the two sentences below can be joined by using a relative clause.

> The antenna improves the reception. The antenna is a long, thin rod on the top of the set.
>
> *which*
> The antenna improves the reception. The ~~antenna~~ is a long, thin rod on the top of the set.
>
> The antenna, *which is a long, thin rod on the top of the set,* improves the reception.

This type of relative clause is called a **nonrestrictive clause.** It adds extra but nonessential information about the noun or noun phrase it modifies. If we remove it from the sentence, the meaning of the sentence does not change in an important way. Nonrestrictive clauses are set off by commas in writing and slight pauses in speech.

## Exercise 16E

Make the second sentence in each pair a nonrestrictive relative clause, and insert it in the blank in the first sentence.

1.     One major control is the on-off control, *which also alters*

*the volume*                                                                     .

(The on-off control also alters the volume.)

2.     An atomic nucleus, _____

_____ , contains protons, neutrons, and

electrons. (An atomic nucleus is the central core of an atom.)

3.     One part of the engine is the spark plugs, _____

_____.

(The spark plugs ignite the gasoline.)

4.     The skin, _____,

has three main layers. (It is the body's largest organ.)

5.     Standard time is calculated from Greenwich, _____

_____.

(Greenwich is located in England.)

## Exercise 16F

Combine each pair of sentences below to make a new sentence. Make the second sentence in each pair a nonrestrictive relative clause. Be sure to insert the relative clause in the right place.

1.     Thin wires produce the heat in an electric blanket.
       The wires are sewn between two layers of material.

*Thin wires, which are sewn between two layers of material, produce the heat in an electric blanket.*

2.     Genes are units of heredity.
       Genes are found in chromosomes.

_____

_____

_____

3.      The layer above the troposphere is the stratosphere.
        The stratosphere extends to an altitude of about thirty-one miles (50 kilometers).

        _____

        _____

        _____

4.      The stomach can hold two to four liters of food.
        It is essentially a collapsible, elastic bag.

        _____

        _____

        _____

5.      Meteors are small fragments of matter moving through the solar system.
        They frequently collide with the earth.

        _____

        _____

        _____

6.      The speed of an electric sewing machine is usually regulated by a foot
        treadle. The foot treadle is located on the floor of the machine.

        _____

        _____

        _____

7.      A supernova is sometimes visible in daylight.
        It is a star of spectacular brightness.

        _____

        _____

        _____

## Exercise 16G

Use each picture to form two sentences with nonrestrictive relative clauses. Your two sentences will emphasize different pieces of information.

1.

**a.** This pen, *which was made in the USA, costs $2.95*

**b.** This pen, *which costs $2.95, was made in the USA.*

2.

**a.** The Mojave Desert _____

**b.** The Mojave Desert _____

3.

**a.** The World Trade Center towers _____

**b.** The World Trade Center towers _____

4.

**a.** Meadville _____

**b.** Meadville _____

5.

TEXAS

RIO GRANDE RIVER

MEXICO

*1885 MILES LONG*

a. The Rio Grande River _____

_____

_____

b. The Rio Grande River _____

_____

_____

## Exercise 16H

Look back at Exercise 16D. Write sentences with relative clauses using at least two pieces of information about the parts.

1. *The stems, which hook on the ears, are thin metal or plastic pieces.*

2. _____

3. _____

4. _____

5. _____

# Student Plan 16
## An AM/FM Radio

**The Parts**

DIAL SCALE

ANTENNA

AM
FM

CORD AND PLUG (OR BATTERIES)

ON-OFF CONTROL

AM  FM

STATION CONTROL

CIRCUITS (INSIDE)

**How They Work**

Imagine that you work as a writer for an electronics firm. They have asked you to explain how a radio works for a handbook for new trainees.

The two pictures on the opposite page show you the major parts of an AM/FM radio and how the parts work together. Discuss the pictures with a partner or a small group. Are there any additional parts you want to include? Make notes with your partner or group and decide on a main idea sentence.

### Helpful vocabulary:

rectangular or square (body)

station

sound

battery-operated

*Main idea sentence\** _____

_____

_____

_____

_____

*You may want to write your main idea sentence after you finish the plan.

*Make Your Plan Here*

# Student Composition 16
## *An AM/FM Radio*

### Stepping Along

**Step 1:** Use your plan to help you write a composition. In addition to your major paragraphs, write an introduction using your main idea sentence, and write a conclusion.

**Step 2:** Exchange compositions with a partner. As you read your partner's composition, think about these questions.

- Is everything in your partner's composition clear to you?

- Is paragraphing correct?

- Is each point sufficiently identified?

- Is each step mentioned in the correct order?

- Can you give your partner at least three suggestions for improvement?

**Step 3:** Talk with your partner about your compositions. Try to agree on improvements you can make.

**Step 4:** Rewrite your composition, making any changes you feel are necessary.

**Further steps:** As directed by your instructor.

# 17
# *The Human Respiratory System*

**The Parts**

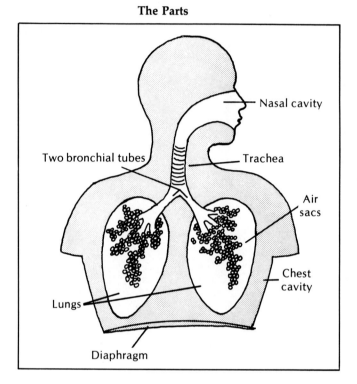

- Nasal cavity
- Two bronchial tubes
- Trachea
- Air sacs
- Chest cavity
- Lungs
- Diaphragm

**How They Work**

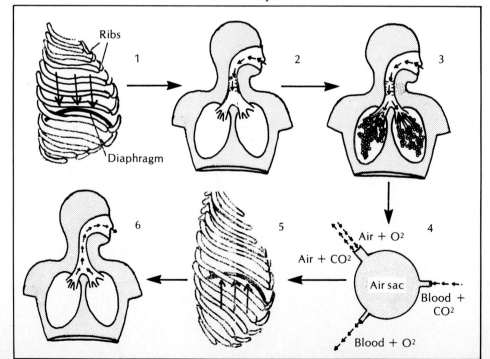

- Ribs
- Diaphragm
- 1
- 2
- 3
- 4
- 5
- 6
- Air + $O_2$
- Air + $CO_2$
- Air sac
- Blood + $CO_2$
- Blood + $O_2$

## PLANNING

A science student wanted to explain the human respiratory system as one of her course projects. She did some research, took some notes, and then organized the notes into this plan. She forgot an important step in II of her plan. *Use the pictures to correct the plan.*

Ⓘ The Parts
  A. Lungs (= millions of air sacs)
  B. Nasal cavity (= system of membrane-lined passages)
  C. Trachea (separates into 2 bronchial tubes)
  D. Bronchial tubes
  E. Diaphragm (= muscle between chest + abdomen)
Ⓘ How They Work
  A. Diaphragm moves down; chest muscles lift ribs.
  B. Air enters nasal cavity.
  C. Air enters trachea.
  D. Bronchial tubes take air to lungs.
    – first to air sacs
    – then blood vessels on sacs take $O_2$ from air and put $CO_2$ into air sacs
  E. Air with $CO_2$ goes out nose.

## WRITING

Here is her final draft. *What are some of the ways she has combined two pieces of information into one sentence?*

### The Human Respiratory System

There are many mechanical systems, but none work better than the systems of the human body. One of these systems is the respiratory system. It consists of the lungs, the nasal cavity, the trachea, the bronchial tubes, and the diaphragm.

The lungs, which consist of millions of tiny air sacs, are located in the chest cavity. The nasal cavity, a system of membrane-lined passages, is in the head. The lungs are connected to the nasal cavity by a tube called the trachea. This tube separates into two bronchial tubes at its lower end. At the bottom of the chest cavity lies the diaphragm, a thick sheet of muscle that separates the chest cavity from the abdominal cavity.

This is how the respiratory system works: The diaphragm moves down, and the chest muscles lift the ribs. When this happens, air enters the nasal cavity through the nose. It passes into the trachea and moves to the lungs through the bronchial tubes. The air then flows into the air sacs, which are covered by blood vessels. These blood vessels take oxygen ($O_2$) from the air and release carbon dioxide ($CO_2$) back into the air sacs. The air that contains carbon dioxide is exhaled through the nose when the diaphragm moves up.

Each part of the respiratory system performs a particular function. We can breathe, then, because the parts work together so well.

## ORGANIZATION

### Explaining the Operation of a Mechanism or Process

When you tell how a mechanism or process works, be sure to put the facts in chronological order. You will also want to use transitions that show this order. Can you list some? For additional help with transitions that show chronological order, look back at Unit 1.

### Exercise 17A

Below are groups of sentences that describe how a mechanism or process works. Place the sentences of each group in proper order by numbering them. Then use the sentences to write a clear, logically ordered paragraph. You may use transitions, combine some of the sentences, change nouns to pronouns, and so on. Study the example.

1.    Rain is formed in the following way.

    __2__    The water vapor is carried upward by the wind.

    __3__    The water vapor cools.

    __1__    Water evaporates.

    __5__    The water vapor condenses into drops and falls as rain.

    __4__    The rising-cooling process continues until the air can no longer hold the vapor.

*Rain is formed in the following way: First, water evaporates. The water vapor is carried upward by the wind and then cools. The rising-cooling process continues until the air can no longer hold the vapor. Finally, the water vapor condenses into drops and falls as rain.*

2.    The digestive system works this way.

    _____    The food passes from the stomach into the small intestine.

    _____    The teeth grind the food.

    _____    The stomach churns the food and adds digestive juice.

    _____    The food passes through the esophagus and into the stomach.

    _____    The food is swallowed.

_____

_____

_____

_____

_____

_____

_____

_____

_____

3.    Coal is formed over a long period of time in the following way.

    _____    The plants begin to rot.

    _____    As the plant debris accumulates, peat is formed.

    _____    The pressure of the sediment slowly compacts the peat.

    _____    The peat is gradually transformed into coal.

    _____    The peat is covered by sediment.

    _____    Generations of plants grow and die in a humid environment.

_____

_____

_____

_____

_____

_____

_____

_____

### Exercise 17B   Irrelevant Sentences

Read the following compositions. Find the sentence in each one that does not support the main idea sentence. Cross it out.

1.

Flashlights come in a range of sizes from pocket-size miniatures to powerful, hand-held searchlights. They all have the same basic parts: a body, a bulb, a socket, a reflector, a window, a spring, and a switch.

First is the body, a hollow cylinder that contains the batteries. These provide the energy for most flashlights. At the top of the body is the bulb, which is inserted in a socket. This is usually attached to the reflector. The reflector, which is made of aluminized plastic or metal, has a parabolic shape. Next is the window that covers the bulb. The spring is at the bottom end of the body and holds the batteries in place. Last is the on-off switch, usually placed on the body.

Here is how the parts work. First, the batteries must be placed inside the body. Next, the switch must be turned on. This causes the electrical current to move from the batteries to the light bulb. When the flashlight is on, the reflector concentrates the light in one direction. Flashlights can be purchased in any hardware store.

Big or small, then, all flashlights function in a similar manner.

2.

Most of us take our ability to speak for granted. However, the production of speech is a complex process. The organs involved are the lungs, the trachea, the larynx, the vocal cords, the pharynx, the mouth, and the nose.

First there are the lungs, which provide the air necessary for voice production. Next is the trachea, a tube that connects the lungs to the larynx. The larynx is shaped like a box and contains the vocal cords. These are two bands of elastic tissue that are horizontal across the larynx and that can be pulled apart or closed. Finally, there is the pharynx, a tube that connects the larynx with the mouth and nose.

Voice is produced in the following way: When we exhale, air from the lungs travels through the trachea to the larynx. When the stream of air passes between the vocal cords, it causes them to vibrate. These vibrations are transmitted through the pharynx, and they emerge from the mouth or nose as voice. Men's voices are usually lower than women's.

Our ability to speak depends on the proper functioning of all these parts.

3.      For plants to make food, several elements must play a role: air, light, stomata, water, roots, and chloroplasts. The process, which takes place mostly in the leaves, is called photosynthesis.

First, plants need air. Air enters the plant through openings in the leaves called stomata. Stomata are located on the surface of leaves between cells. Another important element is light, which contains energy. Water is also necessary. It enters the plant through a network of underground tubes called roots. When you transplant a plant, be careful not to break these off. Last are the chloroplasts, which are oval green bodies located in the leaf cells and containing chlorophyll.

Photosynthesis works like this: Light is absorbed by the chloroplasts, and air enters the leaves through the stomata. At the same time, water is taken in by the roots and travels to the leaves. Energy from the light is used to split the water molecules into hydrogen and oxygen. The hydrogen molecules combine with carbon dioxide from the air and form a sugarlike compound. This is changed to carbohydrates, which the plant uses for food.

In summary, plants need air, light, and water in addition to their own parts for the process of photosynthesis to take place.

# GRAMMAR AND PUNCTUATION

### Exercise 17C   Review of Nonrestrictive Relative Clauses

Fill in each blank with a nonrestrictive relative clause. The relative clause should give the information that is requested in the parentheses.

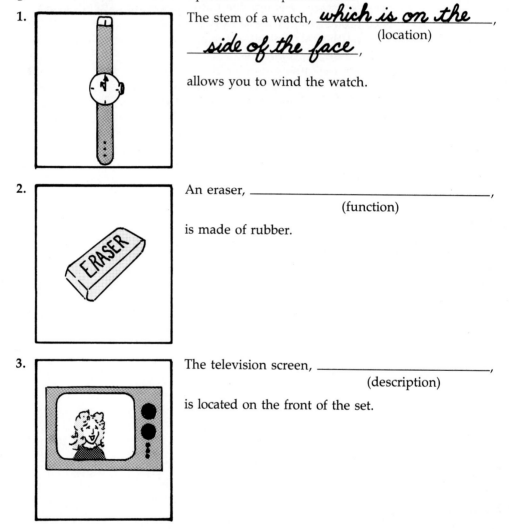

1. The stem of a watch, *which is on the* _____,
(location)
*side of the face*,

allows you to wind the watch.

2. An eraser, _____,
(function)

is made of rubber.

3. The television screen, _____,
(description)

is located on the front of the set.

4.   The paper clip, _____

_____,
(function)
is made of a single piece of twisted metal.

5.   The air sacs, _____,
(location)

exchange $CO_2$ for $O_2$.

## Relative Clauses: Restrictive

Look at the two sentences below.

1. The lungs, which are located in the chest, consist of millions of tiny air sacs.

2. The trachea is a tube $\begin{cases} \text{that} \\ \text{which} \end{cases}$ connects the nasal cavity to the lungs.

In sentence 1, we can remove the relative clause, and the meaning of the sentence does not change in an important way. As you already know, this is called a nonrestrictive clause. Sentence 2 contains a **restrictive clause.** A restrictive clause gives essential information about a noun or noun phrase that sets it apart from the others in the same group. The restrictive clause in sentence 2 tells what makes the trachea different from other tubes in the body, such as the esophagus or the bronchial tubes. We cannot remove a restrictive clause from the sentence because it gives essential information about the noun or noun phrase it modifies. A restrictive clause is *never* set off by commas. When the noun preceding the restrictive clause refers to a thing, the relative clause is introduced with *that* or *which*. *That* is somewhat more common.

## Exercise 17D

Make a restrictive clause from the second sentence in each pair below, and insert it in the blank in the first sentence. You may use either *that* or *which*.

1. The knob *that is on the right of the stove* controls the oven temperature.
   The knob is on the right of the stove.

2. The heart is a muscle _____.
   The muscle pumps blood.

3. The control _____
   regulates the water level in the washing machine.
   The control is labeled "Low," "Medium," and "High."

4. The trachea is a tube _____.
   The tube is made of rings of cartilage.

5. The tachometer is a gauge _____.
   The gauge is marked in rpms.

6. The tube _____
   is called the eustachian tube.
   The tube connects the middle ear to the throat.

Exercise 17E

Make one sentence out of each of the following pairs. Make the second into a restrictive clause.

1. This is the machine.
   The machine grinds meat.

   *This is the machine that grinds meat.*

2. The reflector is a cup-shaped structure.
   This structure concentrates the beam of light.

3. The structure is named the cochlea.
   The structure receives vibrations from the middle ear.

4. The hormone is called secretin.
   The hormone causes the pancreas to secrete.

5. A tendon is a cord of tissue.
   The cord of tissue attaches a muscle to a bone.

6. The ductless gland is called the pituitary gland.
   The ductless gland secretes a growth hormone.

Exercise 17F

Attach a restrictive clause to the noun that is followed by a blank. You can use either *that* or *which*.

1.    Evaporation is the process *that changes a liquid into a vapor*.

2.    The roots are the part of the plant _____
_____.

3.    Animals _____
are called birds.

4.    The face of a clock contains a set of hands _____
_____.

5.    Solar energy is energy _____
_____.

6.    The satellite _____
is the moon.

7.    Soap and detergent are chemical agents _____
_____.

## Relative Clauses: Omitting the Relative Pronoun + the Form of *To Be*

In restrictive and nonrestrictive clauses, the relative pronoun (*which, that,* or *who*) + the form of **to be** (*is, are, was, were*) can usually be dropped.

### <u>EXAMPLES</u>

The nasal cavity, *which is a system of membrane-lined passages,* is in the head.
The nasal cavity, *a system of membrane-lined passages,* is in the head.

The knob *which is on the right* controls the volume.
The knob *on the right* controls the volume.

### Exercise 17G

Look back at Composition 17. Underline once all examples of complete relative clauses. Underline twice all examples of relative clauses where the relative pronoun + *to be* has been omitted.

### Exercise 17H

Cross out the relative pronouns + forms of *to be* wherever possible. (Note: It's not possible to do this in every sentence.)

1. At the bottom of the chest cavity lies the diaphragm, ~~which is~~ a thick sheet of muscle.

2. The heart is a muscle that pumps blood.

3. The antenna—which is a long, thin rod on the top of the set—improves the reception.

4. The knob which is in the middle controls the oven temperature.

5. Silk, which was first discovered in China, is made from the cocoons of silkworms.

6. The antenna, which focuses the picture more clearly, is on top of the set.

7. The nasal cavity is connected to the lungs by a tube which is called the trachea.

8. X-rays—which are invaluable in science, medicine, and industry—are very short electromagnetic rays.

9. Gastric juices are juices in the stomach that digest food.

10. The button that is on the top will turn the computer on.

# Student Plan 17
## A System or Machine

A. Are you interested in a particular machine or system (for example, a bank money machine, a computer system, or a Polaroid camera)? If so, make a plan for a description of it.

OR

B. Suppose you are working for a medical organization, and your boss has asked you to write a brief description of the circulatory system for a brochure on CPR (cardiopulmonary resuscitation) for the general public.

   With a partner or a small group, discuss the pictures. They show you the main parts of the system and how it works. Talk to each other about the parts and the steps, and then write a clear plan of your ideas and a main idea sentence. (You may want to use an encyclopedia or your dictionary for extra help.)

**The Parts**

**How They Work**

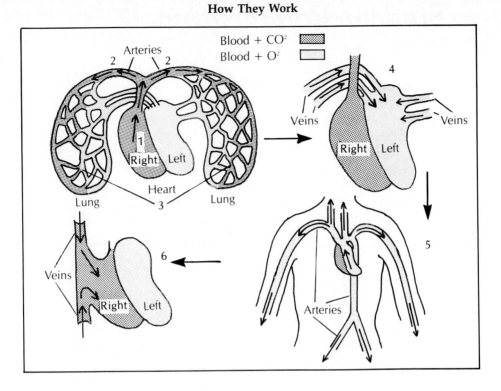

## Helpful vocabulary:

muscle

pump

contract

flow through the arteries and veins

drop $CO_2$

pick up $O_2$

*Main idea sentence* * _____

_____

_____

_____

_____

* You may want to write your main idea sentence after you finish the plan.

*Make Your Plan Here*

# Student Composition 17
## A System or Machine

### Stepping Along

**Step 1:** Use your plan to help you write a composition. In addition to your major paragraphs, write an introduction using your main idea sentence, and write a conclusion.

**Step 2:** Exchange compositions with a partner. As you read your partner's composition, think about these questions.

- Is everything in your partner's composition clear to you?

- Is the paragraphing correct?

- Underline the relative clauses in your partner's composition. Is the punctuation correct? Do the main clause and the relative clause both have verbs?

- Can you give your partner at least three suggestions for improvement?

**Step 3:** Talk with your partner about your compositions. Try to agree on improvements you can make.

**Step 4:** Rewrite your composition, making any changes you feel are necessary.

**Further steps:** As directed by your instructor.

# 18
# *Earthquakes*

**The Components**

**How Earthquakes Occur**

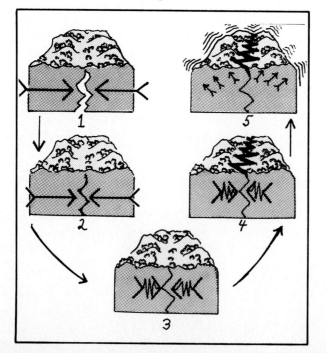

## PLANNING

A student did some research on how earthquakes happen. These are his library notes. *How many components (parts) did he find? How many major steps in the process did he find?*

The Components — large, restless plates (more than 12; each ~ 70 miles thick)
— fault lines (where plates meet)

How It Occurs — Plates bump into each other.
— They lock together.
— Pressure builds up.
— The earth cracks.
— Energy is released in a burst of shocks.

## WRITING

Here is the student's final draft. *What additional information does he include here that was not in his notes? Underline it. How many relative clauses does he use?*

### Earthquakes

Earthquakes occur all over the world. Although we cannot predict them accurately or control their effects, we understand how earthquakes happen. According to scientists, earthquakes can be explained by mobile, platelike segments that cover the surface of the earth.

There are a dozen or more of these large, restless plates, which are each about seventy miles thick. They move slightly each year due to unknown forces deep within the earth. The places where these plates meet are called fault lines. These fault lines are generally earthquake areas.

An earthquake is produced in the following way: First, two or more plates bump against each other with great force. If the plates lock together, as they often do, pressure builds up. When the pressure becomes very strong, the earth cracks. The energy is then released in a burst of shocks, which can often be felt for great distances.

Scientists continue to study these natural disasters. One day, they hope to predict earthquakes before they happen and limit their effect on buildings and people.

# ORGANIZATION

### Exercise 18A   Introductions

Read the following compositions carefully, and write an introduction for each one.

**1.**

_____

_____

_____

_____

_____

The two rows of teeth consist of a large number of metal or plastic pieces that have small protrusions on the top and recesses on the underside. These teeth are held by the two strips of fabric tape. There is also the metal or plastic slide, which can be moved back and forth to open or close the zipper. The small end pieces are located at the ends of the rows of teeth to prevent the slide from coming off.

The zipper works like this: When the slide is pulled in one direction, it draws the two rows together and interlocks the teeth. When the slide is moved in the opposite direction, the teeth separate, and the rows draw apart.

**2.**

_____

_____

_____

_____

_____

The most important element is cream, which is extracted from milk. A high-quality cream will produce a good butter. Other important elements are the various pieces of equipment in the creamery. Large vats equipped with thermostats are used to pasteurize the cream.

Mechanical, cylindrical drums equipped with paddles called baffles are used to churn the cream. Large wooden molds allow the butter to harden.

Butter is made in this way: First, the creameries pasteurize the cream by heating and cooling it in the vats. When the cream reaches just the right temperature, it is put into the drums, where the baffles churn it. This churning causes globules of fat from the cream to cluster together in masses called butter granules. The buttermilk is then drawn off, and the butter is washed with water and salted. Next, it is packed into the molds, where it hardens. Finally, the butter is cut into bricks, wrapped, and shipped to supermarkets.

3. _____

_____

_____

_____

_____

_____

_____

The first element is the seed coat, an outer skin that protects the seed. Inside the seed is the embryo. It contains all the parts necessary for the growth of the plant. Another important element is the endosperm. This consists of one, two, or many seed leaves, which nourish the embryo. Moisture is necessary too. One of its functions is to help dissolve certain food materials in the seed so that these materials can be used for growth. The right temperature is also important for germination. Different seeds need different temperatures, and if the temperature is too high or too low, germination will not occur. The last important element is oxygen. Without it, the chemical changes that accompany growth cannot take place.

A seed germinates in this manner: Moisture softens the seed coat and swells the tissues of the embryo. When the seed coat splits open, the embryo begins to grow. The root part starts growing downward. In many plants, the seed leaves separate and start to rise from the ground. In others, the seed leaves remain in the soil. Finally, the seed leaves dry up, and a pair of true leaves takes their place.

## Exercise 18B   Conclusions

Write a one-sentence conclusion for each short composition in Exercise 18A.

1. _____

   _____

   _____

   _____

   _____

2. _____

   _____

   _____

   _____

   _____

3. _____

   _____

   _____

   _____

   _____

# GRAMMAR AND PUNCTUATION

Exercise 18C   Review of Relative Clauses

Label the second sentence in each pair as either *R* for containing a restrictive clause or *NR* for containing a nonrestrictive clause. Punctuate where appropriate.

1. A rain gauge is used to measure the amount of rain that falls in a certain place or region during a certain period of time.
   *NR* This instrument, which is very simple, consists of a cylinder, a tube, a funnel, and a cover.

2. There are many different kinds of rocks.
   _____ Rocks that were created from molten lava are called volcanic rocks.

3. Picasso painted a great variety of pictures.
   _____ *Guernica* which depicts an incident in the Spanish Civil War is one of the most famous.

4. Different processes can be used to make synthetic natural gas.
   _____ Coal gasification for instance is a process that converts coal into synthetic natural gas.

5. One of the parts of a camera is the box.
   _____ This part which is completely dark inside holds the film.

6. Another part of the camera is the shutter.
   _____ This is the part that controls the amount of light reaching the film.

7. Mother Teresa of Calcutta won the 1979 Nobel Peace Prize.
   _____ The prize which consisted of $193,000 was awarded to her for her work in the slums of Calcutta.

8. The four principal temperature scales are the Fahrenheit, Celsius, Kelvin, and Rankine scales.
   _____ The scales that are the most widely used are the Celsius and the Kelvin.

9. A cell is composed of several different parts.
   _____ The part that surrounds the cell is called the cell membrane.

10. The Aesop fables date from the sixth century B.C.
    _____ These fables which are known all over the world were written by a Greek fabulist.

## Exercise 18D

Following are illustrations and statements that describe (1) the parts of a *flashlight* and (2) the parts that play a role in *voice production*. Practice combining various sentences, using relative clauses. Write at least four sentences for each exercise.

**1.**

The body is a hollow cylinder.

The body contains the batteries.

The batteries provide the energy for the flashlight.

The bulb is attached to the reflector.

The reflector has a parabolic shape.

The reflector is made of aluminized plastic or metal.

The spring is at the bottom end of the body.

The spring holds the battery in place.

a. _____

_____.

b. _____

_____.

c. _____

_____.

d. _____

_____.

**2.**

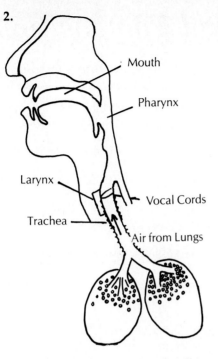

The lungs consist of millions of tiny air sacs.

The lungs provide the necessary air for voice production.

The trachea is a cartilaginous tube.

The trachea connects the lungs to the larynx.

The larynx contains the vocal cords.

The vocal cords lie horizontally across the larynx.

The pharynx is a muscular tube.

The pharynx connects the larynx with the mouth and the nose.

a. _____

_____.

b. _____

_____.

c. _____

_____.

d. _____

_____.

# Student Plan and Composition 18

Develop your own topic, or choose one of the topics below for your final composition. Consider your fellow students as your audience.

1. Describe a simple, small mechanism with which you are familiar, and tell how it works. Have it in front of you as you write.

   Suggestions: *Cigarette lighter* (main parts: case, lighter fluid, wick, flint, flint wheel)

   *Ball-point pen* (main parts: body, cap, push button, spring, ink cartridge)

   *Blender* (main parts: base, motor, blades, glass container, cover, cord with a plug, controls)

2. Describe a part of the body, and explain how it functions. Consult an encyclopedia for help.

   Suggestions: *The eye*
   *The ear*

3. Choose a natural phenomenon. Describe briefly its essential components or elements, and then tell how it occurs. Consult an encyclopedia for help.

   Suggestions: *How hail forms*
   *How stalactites form*
   *How a geyser erupts*
   *How a volcano erupts*

4. *MORE CHALLENGING:* Describe a mechanism that interests you or that relates to your main field of study, and tell how it works. Consult sources (books or knowledgeable people) for extra help.

   Suggestions: *How a solar energy furnace works*
   *How a home computer works*
   *How a printing press works*
   *How a spaceship takes off*

## Stepping Along

**Step 1:** After choosing your topic, take time to think, do research, and write a plan of your major points.

**Step 2:** Write a composition using your plan. Remember to write an introduction and a conclusion.

**Step 3:** Get into groups of three students. Read one another's compositions. As you read your partners' compositions, think about these questions.

- Is the description complete, or has the writer left out a part or a step?

- Is there anything in the composition that is not completely clear to you?

- Can you give the writer three suggestions for improvement?

**Step 4:** Talk with your partners about these questions, and try to agree on improvements each of you can make.

**Step 5:** Rewrite your composition, making any changes you feel are necessary.

**Further steps:** As directed by your instructor.

# Glossary

**Active sentence**  a sentence in which the agent (the one who performs the action) is in subject position

> *The police want that criminal.*

> (The subject, *police,* performs the action.)

**Additional details**  sentences or parts of sentences that give examples to explain major points

**Adverbial**  a word or phrase that tells *when, where, how,* or *how often*

> *She wrote a letter* this morning.

> *When you pass the light, go* left.

> *He yelled* loudly.

> *They* frequently *call.*

**Agent**  a person or thing that performs an action

**Appositive**  a noun or a noun phrase that immediately follows another noun and that explains or defines the noun it follows

> *William Shakespeare,* the famous English dramatist and poet, *was born in 1564.*

**Audience**  person or people or will read what has been written

**Cause**  something that produces a result or an effect

**Chronological order**  an arrangement of events in the order in which they happen in time

**Classification chart**  a treelike diagram that helps in organizing ideas when classifying

| | |
|---|---|
| **Classifying** | organizing ideas or items with similar characteristics into categories |
| **Clause** | a group of words that contains a subject and a verb |
| **Colon** | a punctuation mark (:) that is often used before a list or a series of items |
| | *I met several people: Mr. Burke, Ms. Findley, Dr. Malone, and her daughter.* |
| **Comparative degree** | the form of the adjective that is used when a person, thing, or group s  compared with another person, thing or group |
| | *I am* **taller** *than he is.* |
| | *This car is* **more expensive** *than those.* |
| **Comparing** | thinking or writing about the similarities between two things or people |
| **Composition** | a piece of writing about one central topic |
| **Conclusion** | the final portion of a composition that sums up the major points or makes a judgment based on these major points |
| **Contrasting** | thinking or writing about the differences between two things or people |
| **Dependent clause** | a clause that is used as part of a longer sentence, and that, because it is not grammatically complete, must be connected to a main clause to make sense |
| | *The car will run* **after the battery is replaced.** |
| | **Because the car is not running,** *I will take the bus.* |
| **Direct speech** | the exact words used by a speaker. In writing, direct speech is enclosed by quotation marks. |
| | *The instructor said, "The research paper is due tomorrow."* |
| **Effect** | a result; something that is brought about by a cause or causes |
| **General** | not detailed; not precise |
| | *The word* animal *is more general than the word* dog. |
| **Identify** | define; characterize. You can identify a part of a mechanism by giving its function, its location, or a description of it. |

**Imperative**
a verb form used to give instructions, make requests, and give orders. The base form of the verb is used, but no noun or pronoun is expressed.

> **Write** *clearly.*

> *Please* **come** *here.*

**Indirect object**
the receiver of a direct object

> *Marsha gave* **John** *the book.*

> *Give these copies to* **Ms. Graves.**

**Indirect speech**
a restatement of the words used by a speaker

> *The instructor said that the research paper was due the following day.*

**Introduction**
the beginning portion of a composition that introduces the subject generally. An introduction includes a main idea sentence.

**Introductory phrase**
a phrase that is placed at the beginning of the sentence

> **At the age of sixty-nine,** *Ronald Reagan became president of the United States.*

**Irrelevant**
not connected or not appropriate (An *irrelevant sentence* is a sentence in a composition that is not connected or related to the main idea sentence.)

**Main clause**
a clause that is used as part of a longer sentence but that is grammatically complete and could be a separate sentence

> **The car will run** *after the battery is replaced.*

> *Because the car is not running,* **I will take the bus.**

**Main idea sentence**
a general statement that gives the central idea of a paragraph or a short composition and that is most often placed at the beginning of a piece of writing

**Major points**
those sentences in a composition that directly explain or support the main idea sentence

**Nonrestrictive clause**
a relative clause that adds extra but nonessential information about the noun or noun phrase it modifies. A nonrestrictive clause is *always* set off by commas.

> *My library book* **which is on the desk,** *is due tomorrow.*

> (The relative clause gives extra information about one book.)

**Noun phrase**            a group of words that functions as a noun

  *Lime Street*

  *the hot yellow sand*

**Objective report**       an organized presentation of facts that tells about something that happened

**Outline**                a brief and general plan used to help writers organize their thoughts and ideas before writing

**Paragraph**              a group of related sentences that communicates one central idea

**Parallel**               similar; corresponding

**Passive sentence**       a sentence in which the subject receives the action

  *That criminal is wanted by the police.*

  (The subject, *criminal,* is the receiver of the action.)

**Past continuous tense**  a tense used to refer to an action
  a) that was taking place when another action occurred

  *I **was working** on my paper when you called.*

  b) that was taking place at the same time as another action

  *Abe **was cooking** while I **was gardening.***

**Past tense**             a tense used to refer to something in the past

  *World War II **ended** in 1945.*

  *They **were** very happy.*

**Phrase**                 a grammatical unit of two or more words

**Preposition**            a word that shows the relation between other words

  *Please go **with** Leslie.*

  *Please go **for** Leslie.*

  *Please go **to** Leslie.*

**Present continuous tense**  a tense used for
  a) something that is happening now

  *We **are studying** biology this summer.*

  b) something that will happen in the future

  *Michael **is traveling** to Rome next year.*

**Present tense**  a tense commonly used for
a) a general act or state in the present

> *They* **play** *tennis well.*

> *He* **lives** *near the university.*

b) a habitual action or general truth

> *I* **study** *English every day.*

> *Water* **freezes** *at 0° Centigrade.*

**Pronoun**  a word that stands in place of a noun

> **He** *saw* **her** *at the opera* (rather than
> *Paul* saw *Olivia* at the opera).

**Receiver**  a person or thing that receives an action

**Relative clause**  a clause that modifies and is attached to a noun or a noun phrase

**Restrictive clause**  a relative clause that gives essential information about a noun or noun phrase that sets it apart from others in the same group. A restrictive clause is *never* set off by commas.

> *My library book* **that is on the desk** *is due tomorrow.*
> (The relative clause sets one book apart from others. It tells us which of the books is due tomorrow.)

**Specific**  detailed; precise

> *The word* dog *is more specific than the word* animal.

**Synonyms**  two words that have the same or nearly the same meanings

> *big, large; unhappy, sad*

**Transition**  a word or phrase that is used to connect two ideas

> *Go straight for two blocks.* **Then** *turn right.*

> *She enjoyed the movie. Her husband,* **on the other hand,** *did not.*

**Topic outline**  an outline in which the major points are represented by nouns or noun phrases (topics) rather than complete sentences

# *Index*

# Correction Symbols

| | | | |
|---|---|---|---|
| sp | spelling error | Incorrect: | Go too the post office. |
| | | Correct: | Go to the post office. |
| cap | capitalization error | Incorrect: | I live on main street. |
| | | Correct: | I live on Main Street. |
| p | punctuation error | Incorrect: | I ate an egg and toast. |
| | | Correct: | I ate an egg and toast. |
| wd | wrong word | Incorrect: | I have 21 years old. |
| | | Correct: | I am 21 years old. |
| wf | wrong word form | Incorrect: | He runs slow. |
| | | Correct: | He runs slowly. |
| ⌒ | connect the letters | Incorrect: | People can not drive in the U.S. without a license. |
| | | Correct: | People cannot drive in the U.S. without a license. |
| agr | agreement error | Incorrect: | Jalal always arrive late. |
| | | Correct: | Jalal always arrives late. |
| ref | reference error | Incorrect: | Everybody must do their own work. |
| | | Correct: | Everybody must do his own work. Everybody must do her own work. |
| ⋏ | something is missing here | Incorrect: | They planned to go to restaurant. |
| | | Correct: | They planned to go to a restaurant. |

| ○→ | move word or phrase here | Incorrect: | Sarah (at night) watches TV. |
| | | Correct: | Sarah watches TV at night. |
| T | verb tense error | Incorrect: | I (go) to the movies yesterday. |
| | | Correct: | I went to the movies yesterday. |
| frag | sentence fragment | Incorrect: | Khadiza is always tired. (Because she goes to bed late.) frag |
| | | Correct: | Khadiza is always tired because she goes to bed late. |
| run-on | run-on sentence | Incorrect: | Zaida understands English, she can't speak it. |
| | | Correct: | Zaida understands English, but she can't speak it. |
| trans | transition needed | Incorrect: | Pierre did well on his examination. He failed the course. |
| | | Correct: | Pierre did well on his examination. However, he failed the course. |
| w trans | wrong transition | Incorrect: | Omar plays tennis. (On the other hand,) he plays soccer. |
| | | Correct: | Omar plays tennis. In addition, he plays soccer. |
| / | separate words | Incorrect: | Turn on the light. |
| | | Correct: | Turn on the light. |
| X | omit this | Incorrect: | Dang he is sick and can't come to class. |
| | | Correct: | Dang is sick and can't come to class. |
| [?] | not clear | This symbol is used when your instructor does not know what you mean. | |
| ¶ | new paragraph | This symbol is used when indentation is needed to indicate a new paragraph. | |
| no ¶ | no new paragraph | This is used to indicate that a new paragraph should not be started here. | |